Werner and Susanne Lantermann
with Matthew M.

Amazon
Parrots

Everything about Purchase, Care,
Feeding, and Housing

Filled with Full-color Photographs
Illustrations by Fritz W. Köhler

BARRON'S

2 CONTENTS

Before You Get an Amazon 5

Amazons as Pets 5

What to Consider Before Buying 5

One Bird or a Pair? 6

Children and Amazons 7

Amazons and Other Pets 7

Vacation Care 7

Advice for Buying 9

Where You Can Get Amazons 9

Before You Buy 9

Age Determination 11

Sex Determination 11

Formalities When Buying 14

Two Serious Threats to Birds 15

Housing 17

The Cage 17

Room Aviaries 17

Fittings for Cages and Room Aviaries 18

Freestanding Perches and Climbing Trees 19

Outdoor Shelter and Flight Cage 22

Acclimation and Care 25

Taking the Amazon Home 25

Acclimation 25

Placement in an Aviary 26

Making Your Parrot Hand-Tame 26

How Amazons Learn to "Speak" 27

Play and Activities 28

Flying Free in the House 29

Table: Dangers for Your Amazon 30

HOW-TO: Proper Care 34

Proper Diet 37

The Basic Diet 37

Sprouted Feed 37

Fruit and Green Feed 38

Animal Feed 39

Inappropriate Food for Parrots 39

Table Scraps 39

Breeding Food 39

Vitamins and Minerals 39

Drinking Water 42

Proper Feeding 42

A Sample Daily Diet for Your Amazon 43

Health and Illness 45

Common Illnesses 45

Parrot Fever (Psittacosis) 49

HOW-TO: Caring for Your Sick Amazon 50

Breeding Amazons 53

The Washington Endangered Species Convention 53

Breeding to Preserve the Species? 53

Legal Requirements for Amazon Breeding 54

Maintenance Conditions for Breeding 54

Courtship and Mating 56

Egg Laying and Brooding 56

Hatching and Rearing the Young 57

Hand-feeding 58

Hybrid Offspring 61

Bird Shows 62

Understanding Amazons 65

How Amazons Live
Together in Nature 65

Important Behavior
Patterns of Amazons 66

**Popular Amazon
Species 73**

Some Facts About
Amazons 73

Frequently Kept Amazon
Species 74

Appendix 82

Parrot Species in
Danger of Extinction 82

Extinct Species 83

Information 84

Index 86

BEFORE YOU GET
AN AMAZON

Amazons as Pets

Amazon parrots—usually called Amazons for short—are among the most popular of the large parrots. Their popularity is all too easy to understand, for most parrots—when kept as single birds—allow themselves to be quickly tamed, usually rapidly bond closely to their keeper, and many of them have a pronounced talent for mimicry. In contrast to many others of the large parrots, they get used to living in a cage or an aviary virtually without problems. Also, their appealing ways and their "great intelligence" fascinate the parrot fancier. All these good qualities, which show that the Amazons are adaptable parrots, unfortunately often lead to spur-of-the-moment buying. However, we must urgently warn you against an unconsidered purchase. Only an Amazon that is kept well and properly will develop into a pet that will give you pleasure. And always remember that many pet birds are devoted to only one person, or will tolerate attention from men *or* from women but not both.

Never forget that Amazons can bite very hard if excited or teased; they are not recommended as children's pets (see page 7).

There is also another important reason for not keeping Amazons under inappropriate conditions, one that should furthermore

The Cuban Amazon (**Amazona leucocephala**).

induce you to think of keeping two and raising its young, rather than keeping only one: The survival of most Amazon species in nature is greatly endangered. At this time, 19 of the 27 Amazon species are designated severely endangered or threatened with total extinction by the Washington Endangered Species Convention (Appendix I). All other species are legally regulated by animal protection laws. This means that due to recent laws, birds are no longer imported into the United States. Importation is controlled by CITES, the Convention of International Trade in Endangered Species.

What to Consider Before Buying

Before you get an Amazon, consider carefully whether you can satisfy its requirements for life. You particularly need to weigh the following points:

✔ The parrot needs much attention from its caretaker, particularly if it is alone and has no companion.

✔ It must have freedom of movement—a climbing branch and freedom to exercise.

✔ It needs opportunities to play with objects.

✔ Parrots can live to be very old, and you will be caring for the parrot for many years.

✔ Most important of all, if Amazons are going to be kept in a house: Amazons soil things; it can't be avoided.

✔ Parrots can scream very loudly, which in some circumstances can lead to difficulties with noise-sensitive neighbors—find out ahead of time if the neighbors (and also the land-lord!) will tolerate a parrot being kept nearby. It is advised that you get a written statement.
✔ Will the Amazon get along with pets you have already (see page 7)?
✔ People who are allergic to feathers or feather dust should not under any circum-stances keep parrots; if in doubt, consult your physician before you buy a bird.

Note: If you want to keep Amazons in an outdoor aviary—and eventually breed them—you should read about this in the chapter on Breeding Amazons (see page 53).

Most wild-caught adult birds will need some time before they start breeding. They first have to adjust, and in time they will become less nervous. With each year that passes, the pro-portion of avian-bred to wild-caught birds increases.

Since it is no longer legal to bring wild-caught birds into the United States, this will not be a problem; however, the number of ille-gal (smuggled) birds will most likely increase.

Those birds are easily recognizable as they are not wearing the proper leg band—or they wear no band at all. It is obviously illegal to have those birds in your possession.

One Bird or a Pair?

You really should settle this question before you buy, but at least know why it is so impor-tant for keeping a parrot.

The single bird: The novice parrot keeper will surely begin with a single Amazon. Most likely he or she will try to tame it and teach it to "speak." It is indisputable that for a certain length of time—at least until they become sexually mature—single birds, with constant attention from the keeper, remain in psychological balance and act like ideal house pets. However, with the onset of sexual maturity—in about the fourth or fifth year of life—many single birds exhibit some conspicuous behavioral changes. The parrot is restless; female Amazons frequently lay infertile eggs on the cage floor. Constant frustration can cause the beginnings of feather plucking as well as other psychological disturbances.

The pair: Anyone who is closely acquainted with the way of life and the behavior patterns of large parrots will have to admit that in the long run the human as substitute mate cannot fulfill all the social requirements of a parrot. Living together as mates is part of the natural behavior pattern of the Amazon and that of most other large parrots. Even if you cannot decide to get a pair at first, you should not rule out this possibility for some time in the future. Parrots who get along well together

Social grooming: Two Amazons that get along well with each other groom each other's feathers repeatedly and thoroughly.

show fascinating behavior in their companionship, which certainly compensates the parrot owner for the fact that the second bird has taken over his or her role as partner. This does not mean at all that once-tamed and "speaking" parrots will turn away from their keeper or become mute or silent.

Note: For parrot fanciers who are away from home most of the day and therefore can give little attention to their parrots, keeping a pair is the only thing that can be considered, if indeed parrots should be kept at all.

Children and Amazons

Babies and small children should never be left unsupervised with a parrot. Parrots can sometimes be very jealous, especially if babies or small children contest their special place in the family. It is possible that they may attack the child and injure it with their sharp claws and powerful beak. After the birth of a baby, you must see to it that you do not neglect the Amazon, for in most cases it will soon get used to the newcomer. But, as we have said, *never* leave the two of them together unsupervised.

Older children and adolescents can gradually become familiar with the habits of an Amazon. They learn with time how to get along properly with the parrot.

Amazons and Other Pets

Dogs and cats: As a rule, Amazons easily get used to a cat or a dog after a short time. Both "parties" learn quickly to accept each other. Basically, a large dog or a cat, too, is physically overwhelming to an Amazon, but one should by no means underestimate the defense capabilities of a well-armed parrot. For the first few days it's best if you carefully watch the animals until you are sure that both have come to an agreement or at least will leave each other in peace. Nevertheless, if you happen to have a hunting dog, be very alert, as these breeds can become very excited at the sight of a tame, free-flying Amazon in the house.

Small mammals: Amazons can be dangerous to hamsters, guinea pigs, mice, or gerbils if they actually bite them. Watch how your animals get along with each other; in some cases, keeping them in separate rooms is advisable.

Smaller birds: Some Amazons simply ignore smaller birds; but many times the meeting can also be fatal for the smaller bird.

Note: There are no general rules for the way different pets get along together. Close friendships are just as possible as deadly enmity. One must often simply try to find out what works and what doesn't. In any case, you should always be alert to be able to intervene and help protect your pets if necessary.

Vacation Care

Before you get a parrot as a pet, you must decide who is going to take care of the bird while you are on vacation or if you become ill. Most people find a family member or a neighbor who will take over the feeding and the essential care duties. But remember that a single bird also needs attention and conversation during your absence. Often other parrot fanciers in an area will take turns being "vacation stand-ins." It's advantageous if Amazons can remain in their familiar surroundings. If necessary you can also take your parrots to the local pet dealer who will take them into his or her keeping for a fee; ask ahead of time whether the pet dealer has room and enough time to board a parrot.

ADVICE FOR BUYING

Where You Can Get Amazons

Pet stores: The novice parrot keeper, especially, should first look for his or her new house pet in a well-managed pet store. Most of the Amazons sold there were caught in the wild, in their native habitats, and sent on order, by plane, to a wholesaler (a direct importer). There the parrots went through a legally established quarantine period (30 days at this time), during which they underwent psittacosis immunization (see page 49). The quarantine stations were tended and supervised by veterinarians; the birds were fed a medicated feed as required by the U.S. Public Health Service. After this procedure, which was very stressful for the parrot, the birds were released to the individual dealers. Parrots are no longer imported into the United States from the wild. You may be able to purchase an occasional older parrot that was imported years ago, before the ban on importation took place, but the average person will only have access to parrots bred in the United States.

Since importation ceased, there has been a great increase in breeding parrots in the United States, and buying one of these birds offers many advantages: They have not gone through quarantine with its regimes of heavy medication, and, in addition, if they have been hand-fed they will be quite tame. Best of all, by buying a domestic bird, we are not depleting the parrots found in the wild.

Breeders: Many parrot fanciers would like to get their Amazons from a breeder. Unfortunately, at this time there are not many Amazon breeders. There are dedicated Amazon fanciers who erratically and often purely by accident succeed in raising several young birds, but there can be no talk of breeding in any real sense (see page 53). The total number of Amazon babies born in the United States and Europe can only be guessed at. The possibility of getting a locally raised Amazon is conceivable, especially in such states as Florida and California. Sometimes, though, pet dealers and the few "breeders" place advance orders for all the expected broods for the next year. The advantages to having an Amazon born in human captivity are obvious. For one thing, buying the bird does not decimate the natural supply; for another, the Amazon is already well adapted to our climate. Such a parrot is less shy of humans because of its experiences. It is to be hoped that in the future the number of Amazons born in captivity will increase markedly.

Parrots are skillful climbers. A Yellow-naped Amazon (Amazona ochrocephala auropalliata) *and a bright scarlet Ara* (Ara macao) *in their natural habitat.*

Before You Buy

Give yourself lots of time to buy your Amazon. Make certain first that the living quarters of the parrots you are offered are clean and that the food supply is properly arranged. In addition, you should look carefully at the Amazons. It is certainly not at all easy to judge the health condition of an Amazon, but some essential points to look for can help you to come to a fairly certain judgment.

Behavior: For a while, observe the parrot you are interested in from a distance. It should be lively (naturally, the frequent rest periods are the exception), occasionally climbing around in the cage; no forced movements should be visible; while resting crouching on one foot or while eating, the parrot should be able to take large pieces of food in one claw while sitting on the other without wavering and with no loss of balance.

Appearance: Now observe the parrot close up. Its eyes should be clear and shining, the

nostrils dry and clear, the area around the nose also dry and not crusted with little pieces of feather. If this is not the case, you should avoid buying it. Also not recommended is the purchase of an Amazon on which you can discern external wounds or beak irregularities such as broken pieces of beak or anomalies of position of upper and lower mandible. However, missing toes, toe segments, or claws are beauty flaws that, except for drastic examples, should not force you to give up the idea of buying.

A shining, smooth, colorful plumage suggests that the Amazon is healthy. In the past, all newly imported parrots had some degree of imperfect and rumpled plumage due to the stress of being transported in a small traveling cage.

Feces: In a healthy parrot the droppings consist of a partly olive-green and a partly white urine portion of medium-firm consistency. Deviations from this in color, and also watery droppings, can indicate an illness of the intestinal tract. Also, there should be no crust of feces attached to the vent—the opening from which the parrot excretes—as this may indicate loose stools. However, food changes and unusual experiences such as stress, for example, can produce symptoms of diarrhea in a parrot for a short time without its being actually sick (see page 45).

Sleeping posture. Healthy parrots sleep on one leg; the other leg is pulled into the belly feathers; the head is turned 180 degrees to the rear and tucked into the back feathers.

The nutritional condition: Ask the seller to catch the parrot you have chosen so that you can check how well nourished the bird is. Carefully feel the breast musculature with your hand—fleshy muscle webs on both sides of the readily palpable ridge of the breastbone indicate a well-nourished parrot. Individual muscle parts with a sharply prominent breastbone are typical of a poorly nourished bird. Inexperienced parrot keepers should not buy such a bird.

The wings: If you hold the Amazon in your hand, it is easy to check the integrity of the pinions to see the degree of cutting of the wing feathers, which has usually been done in the country of origin. Pay particular attention to the outside joint, the third finger of the middle hand bone. Occasionally, with too drastic cutting methods, the feathers will no longer grow in this place and the parrot can no longer fly.

Age Determination

The exact age of an Amazon cannot be established except in the case of the captive-bred bird. With a newly imported parrot one could begin with the idea that it must be at least six months old, if you consider the nestling period and add in the time spent in the camp of the South American trapper and in quarantine. If you are dealing with a retail store you must also figure in the time the parrot has spent there. But it is possible that the parrot is substantially older, for adult parrots are also captured and brought into trade.

Being able to ascertain the age of a newly acquired Amazon is obviously of practical importance to a parrot owner. There are a number of fairly reliable clues for telling a juvenile bird up to about two years of age.

Bill: Young parrots have smooth, shiny bills; in older birds the accumulation of thin, horny plates—parrots' bills never stop growing—give the bill a less regular appearance.

Legs and toes: The skin pattern on the legs and toes becomes coarse with age, and the epidermis grows thicker. In fully grown birds, the horny plates are clearly visible on the toes, whereas these plates are still very fine in younger birds.

Eyes: In many Amazons, eye color helps determine age. Almost all juvenile parrots have dark (gray, brown, or black) irises that usually lighten with age. The change is particularly clear in Amazons. With increasing age, the eye color becomes more distinct.

Size and plumage: Juveniles are usually smaller than adults of their species; their plumage is more muted, and the markings grow bigger and deepen in color.

Reminder: At this point, the best we can do is to distinguish in general between immature and adult birds. It would be useful to be able to tell the difference between, say, a three-year-old and an eight-year-old bird. Even to make an educated guess of this sort, however, takes extensive experience and the chance to compare many birds.

Sex Determination

With two exceptions, Amazon males and females are not distinguishable from one another by any external features. Most of the external marks that are vigorously discussed in the parrot literature and among parrot experts are much too uncertain to be relied on.

The Red-spectacled Amazon (**Amazona pretrei**) *is native to southernmost Brazil.*

The Orange-winged Amazon (**Amazona amazonica**).

The Vinaceous Amazon (Amazona vinacea) *is a nice bird that tends to be very quiet.*

For the keeper of a single bird, it is unimportant what sex the Amazon is, since males as well as females have the same "aptitude" for becoming good house pets.

Endoscopy and Feather Chromosome Sexing

On the other hand, for the breeder it is important to determine the sex of his or her birds to avoid years of failed breeding attempts. Laparoscopy (endoscopy of the abdominal cavity) has so far shown itself to be a relatively low-risk method. It can be done by many veterinarians and bird clinics for a fee, with nearly 100 percent success. The Amazon must be anesthetized; a small incision under the bottom rib permits passage of an endoscope (a tiny mirror with a lighting apparatus), with which the sex organs can be visualized directly. As a rule, there are no complications of any sort from the anesthetic, and after awakening the bird is quickly back to sitting on its perch.

Important: Debilitated, sick, and quarantined birds should not undergo endoscopy.

An even safer method, however, is Feather Chromosome Sexing, using a blood feather, which is a feather that is still growing and therefore has blood in the shaft. The blood feather is removed from the bird to be sexed. Then the pulp is removed from the shaft and a cell culture is grown from the pulp. All that is required is one blood quill that must be kept sterile and must reach the laboratory—for nearby addresses, consult your avian veterinarian—within 24 hours.

After seven to ten days, enough cells will have grown in the culture to enable a chromosome preparation to be made. The chromosomes are then analyzed, thus determining sex

and also whether the bird possesses any chromosomal defect. For example, some birds are genetically intersex—neither male nor female—and are therefore sterile. Outwardly normal, this could never be discovered in any other manner.

Amazon Species with External Sex Characteristics

Two Amazon species, the yellow-lored Amazon (Amazona xantholora) and the white-fronted Amazon (Amazona albifrons), allow distinction between the sexes because of their plumage color. The yellow-lored Amazon is rarely seen in trade, so for the majority of parrot keepers only the differential markings of the white-fronted Amazon are of any importance. Male white-fronted Amazons have red at the front edge of the wing and a red wing speculum, whereas the females as a rule are pure green in this area.

Nevertheless, young females with individual red feathers at the wing front are occasionally described in the literature.

Formalities When Buying

When you buy the Amazon you have carefully chosen and observed, there are still some formalities to undergo.

✔ In Europe the Amazon is required to wear an official leg band with a number, which the seller must note in the records together with your address.

✔ In a European pet store, as a matter of course, you will receive a proper bill on which the band number is also noted. If you buy in another place, be sure to ask the seller for a bill that contains the name and address of the seller and buyer, the sale price, and the band number.

✔ If, according to the pet dealer, a sex determination of the Amazon has been made, ask that this be indicated on your receipt.

Two Serious Threats to Birds

As a bird owner, you should know the symptoms of exotic *Newcastle disease,* the devastating disease of poultry and other birds. If your birds show signs of incoordination and breathing difficulties, or if there should be any unusual die-off among them, contact your local veterinarian or animal health official immediately. Place dead birds in plastic bags, and *refrigerate* them for submission to a diagnostic laboratory. Keep in mind that this disease is highly contagious, and you should isolate any newly purchased birds for at least 30 days. Although exotic Newcastle disease is not a general health hazard, it can cause minor eye infections in humans.

If you're tempted to buy a bird you suspect may have been smuggled into the United States, don't! Smuggled birds are a persistent threat to the health of birds and poultry flocks in this country. Indications are that many recent outbreaks of exotic Newcastle disease were caused by birds entering the United States illegally. If you have information about the possibility of smuggled birds, report it to any U.S. Customs office or call APHIS at Hyattsville, Maryland, (301) 436-8061.

HOUSING

The Cage

The majority of Amazons are kept in a cage in the home. Their cage must not become a constricting prison, so you should only buy a cage in which they feel comfortable.

Size: The parrot cages that are generally available, with dimensions of 16 × 16 × 23 inches (40 × 40 × 60 cm) or 16 × 16 × 31 inches (40 × 40 × 80 cm), are much too small for keeping even a single parrot. These cages may be useful during the brief acclimation period or for caring for an ailing Amazon, but there is no question of their being a permanent accommodation. To provide for the Amazon's need for movement, you should choose one of the cages that is offered as an indoor aviary in pet stores. They are 39 to 59 inches (100–150 cm) high and have a floor surface of about 23 × 39 inches (60 × 100 cm). There are many models, so you can certainly find an appropriate Amazon cage that will fit in with your décor, if that is important to you.

Shape: A parrot cage should have a rectangular or square bottom; round cages are unsuitable.

The cage mesh: Since Amazons like to climb, the cage bars should be horizontal on at least two sides of the cage. The spaces between the bars should be at least 0.6 inches (15 mm) wide and at most 1 inch (25 mm), and the bars

The Tres Marias Amazon (**Amazona ocrocephala tresmariae**).

should be thick enough so that even a large Amazon can't bend or bite through them.

Floor surface: A pan for catching droppings that can be pulled out of the bottom like a drawer makes the work of regular cleaning much easier. In some cages a wire grate is fastened about an inch (a few centimeters) above the floor, which is supposed to keep the Amazons away from their excrement and the food droppings in order to decrease the risk of illness. However, this floor grating keeps the birds from being able to pick up small stones from the sand litter, and these stones promote their digestion. If you don't want to remove the grill, it's essential that you provide a good bird sand or grit in a separate food dish. Failure to get these essential little stones or a proper parrot grit over a protracted period of time can have serious consequences for the Amazon and may even result in its death.

Cage door: It must be large enough so that you can reach into the cage easily, and the bird can climb in and out without any difficulty.

Room Aviaries

Room aviaries with a height of at least 70 inches (180 cm) and a floor of at least 39 × 59 inches (100 × 150 cm) are recommended for Amazons. An accommodation of this size is suitable for both a single bird and a pair of Amazons.

Fasten a nest box firmly to the back wall, which usually consists of a solid piece of wood.

The available cages range from ready-made room-sized aviaries to components and mesh of various different measurements. It's best to take the advice of the pet dealer who will

A well-equipped parrot cage. Two Amazons can comfortably live in one of these if they have regular opportunities to fly.

show you the manufacturer's catalogs and help you with the choice of a suitable cage. Parrot keepers who are handy can of course expend some effort and build their own large room aviary of galvanized square mesh 0.6 × 0.6 inches (15 × 15 mm) or stronger; see also Outdoor Shelter and Flight Cage, page 22.

Fittings for Cages and Room Aviaries

Perches: The perches should be of wood—beech, pine, willow, manzanita, except cherry—either round or square with rounded edges, and should be 1 to 1½ inches (25 to 35 mm) thick. Highly recommended are various-sized branches of fruit trees that have not been sprayed; in any case, be sure to take the precaution of scrubbing with hot water. These are good because their rough surface will wear down the claws of the Amazon naturally so they won't have to be cut. Besides, different sizes of branches offer the parrots a kind of "foot exercise" that helps to prevent laming of their feet.

Food and drinking containers: Standard plastic or pottery dishes are usually included in the price of a cage; you can get replacements or other dishes—there should be three, see page 42—in the pet store. Plastic dishes should be changed after about two years, because by that time they can no longer be cleaned thoroughly. Don't place food and drinking dishes under the perches where they can be fouled by falling droppings. Mount dishes that stand on a feeding shelf—often the case in large aviaries—so that the parrots can't knock them to the floor. The stainless-steel food and water dishes in a special holder, available in the pet store, are very practical for cages and aviaries.

Playthings: Climbing ropes, chains with large links, fresh branches for gnawing, clean stones that the birds can take in their beaks but can't swallow, and parrot toys made of wood, available in the pet store, supply the single bird and also aviary birds with variety and chances for play.

Placement of Cages and Room Aviaries

A parrot home should not be constantly moved back and forth; it should be in a place that is protected from drafts, and should not be exposed to cigarette smoke or cooking odors.

A quiet corner in the living room that is bright, airy, draft-free, and occasionally sunny is appropriate. Never put the cage in the middle of the room; without the back of a wall or a corner, the birds feel insecure.

The cage must not stand on the floor unless it has legs that keep it above floor level. Amazons feel most comfortable and secure if they view their surroundings from a somewhat elevated lookout such as eye level.

You should always have the cage of a single bird in the most used room so that the parrot can take part in family life and not be bored. Although in many homes the kitchen is a hub of activity, it is *not* a good location for your parrot's cage because of fumes, hot stoves, and other dangers.

A freestanding parrot perch: Adding natural branches to a standard pet store perch makes it much more interesting for the parrot.

Freestanding Perches and Climbing Trees

Acclimated, hand-tame Amazons can be kept for hours, even in some cases constantly, on a perch or climbing tree outside the cage. It's a welcome change for the Amazon, and the parrot owner can maintain good contact with the bird and enjoy watching its acrobatics.

The Orange-winged Amazon (**Amazona amazonica**) *lives in the damp woods of northern South America.*

Cuban Amazons can be found in Cuba (although they are rare now), the Bahamas, the Cayman Islands, and the Isle of Pines.

The Double yellow-headed Amazon (Amazona ochrocaphala oratrix).

Freestanding perches are available ready-made at the pet store. Hobbyists who want to offer their parrot more than the commercially available smooth round rod can make the freestanding perch even more varied by means of natural branches (see drawing on page 19).

For a climbing tree you need a forked piece of branch or a small tree as well as a sand-filled container such as a cement or wooden planter. The branch sections or tree must be firmly fastened in the container with metal corners.

Keeping the Amazon on a climbing tree or a freestanding perch is very much to be recommended, but as a rule you have to supervise the bird. Amazons that are able to fly will gladly undertake expeditions through the house or apartment and can do damage or be injured themselves. Amazons whose wings have been clipped on one side very seldom leave the freestanding perch or the climbing tree voluntarily, probably because in the beginning they experienced, often painfully, what happened when they tried to fly with only one wing intact.

For an outdoor climbing tree, fruit trees are eminently suitable. The tree must be shortened to a height that you can see over. However, fruit trees that you want to keep should not be subjected to the beaks of Amazons. Keeping the bird outside can be considered only in good weather, with wing-clipped Amazons, and under supervision, for Amazons can fall from trees or climb down and subsequently "run away," or else become the victims of lurking cats or the neighbors' dogs. Therefore, only tame birds should be allowed to climb outside trees and *with their wings clipped.* Remember, many parrots are lost while outside, climbing and playing and fluttering with clipped wings. Wing feathers also grow back and the parrot

may regain its ability to fly much quicker than you thought possible.

Outdoor Shelter and Flight Cage

If you want to keep parrots, and perhaps even breed them, we strongly recommend setting up an outdoor aviary with an attached flight cage. In the literature (see Information, page 84) you will find books that tell you how to build this kind of an enclosure, or you can commission one from a local building firm.

Building the Bird Shelter

To make your planning easier, there are some basic things you need to consider when building an aviary:

✔ Find out about local building regulations and whether a building permit is necessary.

✔ In our experience an aviary with stone walls is best suited for keeping parrots (wood has some drawbacks—for instance, because of the "gnawing fever" of many Amazons).

✔ The shelter needs a cement foundation.

✔ Don't forget to plan for windows (preferably of glass brick) and doors (inquire about door dimensions ahead of time).

✔ The roof is best made of glass brick or wood. Tar paper works well to make the roof watertight.

✔ For Amazon parrots the house must be slightly heated in winter; to cut down on the cost of heating, insulation is recommended.

✔ The fly-through to the flight cage is created by swivel-mounted glass-brick windows or tin sliding panels.

✔ Furnishing the shelter with broad-spectrum light, several humidity-proof wall sockets, a heat source, and running water attached to a drain is highly recommended.

✔ The size of the protected area: A ground surface of 39 × 39 inches (1 × 1 m) and a height of 59 to 79 inches (1.5–2 m) is enough for an Amazon pair; the space should be no smaller than this.

✔ The equipment of the interior room consists of a feeding shelf with inset dishes, several perches, and a nesting box.

The Open Flight Cage

The flight cage should be attached to the shelter, so that in periods of bad weather or in winter the parrots can access their inner room without hindrance. Here is some information about building a flight cage:

✔ It is advisable to lay a cement foundation— about 23 to 31 inches (60–80 cm) deep to keep out rats and other uninvited "guests."

✔ For Amazons a length of 79 to 118 inches (2–3 m) is sufficient; the width is determined by the width of the shelter.

✔ Welded, galvanized steel pipes are best to use for the framework of the flight cage. This will ensure ample sturdiness.

✔ A part of the flight cage will be roofed with galvanized tin or plastic sheets, the remainder covered with wire fencing (galvanized rectangular mesh, mesh width 0.5 × 1 inch [12.5 × 25 mm], 0.7 × 0.7 inch [17.5 × 17.5 mm], or 1 × 1 inch [25 × 25 mm], wire gauge at least 0.04 inch [1 mm]).

✔ We recommend paving stones as flooring. A solid cement floor leads to pooling of water during extended rainy spells, and within a short time, floors of natural ground are so full of pathogens that hygienic parrot maintenance can no longer be guaranteed.

✔ At least two perches should be installed in a flight cage—depending on its size—and placed as far away from each other as possible to leave room for flying; there should also be a branched climbing and gnawing tree as well as a birdbath. Even Amazons that get along well with each other need their space!

ACCLIMATION AND CARE

Taking the Amazon Home

A newly acquired Amazon should be transported to its future home as quickly as possible. Wooden boxes or firm cardboard cartons with dimensions of about 10 × 10 × 18 inches (25 × 25 × 45 cm) are good carrying containers.

For short journeys a cardboard carton will do; it must have airholes punched in it.

For longer trips you need a stable carrier, which should contain a perch and a filled food dish, and place several pieces of fruit in the carrying cage instead of a water dish. In this way you will not run the risk of soaking the bird with water if the vehicle it is in lurches or turns suddenly. Special animal-carrying crates with a wire-covered opening for ventilation are ideal; these are available in a pet store or you can build the carrier yourself.

It is important that the traveling cage be closed—except for the wire-covered ventilation hole—so that the bird does not become terrified by the constantly changing impressions during a journey by bus, train, or car, and begin to flutter around wildly in the carrier. Cages are not suitable for transporting parrots for this reason. The bird can injure itself badly by flapping around.

Acclimation

Once you have arrived home, release the parrot from its traveling carrier into the cage

*The Imperial Amazon (**Amazona imperialis**) is the largest species of Amazon parrots.*

that is standing ready, in which the food dishes are already filled and the floor is covered with sand. Open the carrier and hold the opening in front of the cage door in such a way that the parrot cannot escape. If it still manages to escape, whatever you do, avoid going on a "wild chase" after the new arrival, which is still doubtless frightened from the journey. You will only succeed in getting the anxious fugitive into its new house with calm, patience, and perhaps some unusual delicacy. Leave your Amazon completely at peace for the first few days, making sure it takes enough food. In the beginning, offer the bird familiar food (ask the dealer about this when you buy it) and only later slowly correct the nutritional palette (see Proper Diet, page 37).

Note: Also put aviary birds in a cage to get acclimated at first; never put them with other birds immediately, either with those of their own species or with others.

First Fecal Examination

After the Amazon has lived alone for several days and has become calmer, and its feces have gone from nervously induced diarrhea to a normal, firm consistency, take a fecal sample. In the evening, spread a plastic sheet under the perch; remove it the next morning with the droppings, and immediately place the fecal sample in a clean glass jar and take the sample to the veterinarian for examination. If any treatment is necessary, follow the advice of the veterinarian exactly.

Placement in an Aviary

A newcomer may be placed in an already occupied cage only when the first fecal examination shows it to be free of infection or when any necessary treatment is successfully concluded. This is necessary to protect the older inhabitants of the aviary from contagious illness. Furthermore, the bird must be completely healthy, because now a period of further stress is beginning for it as it experiences change and gets used to its new surroundings. It must become familiar with new relationships, with partner birds or rivals, and, if necessary, must fight for its ranking and access to the food dish. In any case, you must devote special attention to it in the first months—just as for a single bird—in order to be able to intervene as quickly as possible at the first signs of indisposition.

Making Your Parrot Hand-Tame

An Amazon becomes accustomed the most rapidly of all the parrot species to the presence of human beings and will usually quickly become quiet and comfortable in the cage. The acclimation phase and the period just after it, when the parrot spends its time exclusively in the cage, are most opportune for beginning hand-taming, but give the parrot a few days at first to get used to its new surrounding. Besides, it should already recognize your voice and know that you pose no danger. These are important prerequisites for hand-taming.

Steps in Taming

The first step: When the Amazon no longer withdraws from you and now watches its human companions with interest, it will not be long until it will take the first treat out of your hand. To begin with, put the treat into the cage. You must move cautiously and quietly so that the bird does not become frightened and peck at your hand with its beak. In time, the hand that offers the treat will become less and less feared, and at some point you will be able to playfully scratch your Amazon for the first time without its recoiling or even biting. After several weeks—it can take longer with some parrots—the Amazon will accept the hand as the substitute for the social plumage care that parrots otherwise carry out for each other, and sooner or later it will hold its head next

A parrot transport box for the do-it-yourself builder. You'll need ½ inch (10–15 mm) thick plywood and narrow mesh wire caging. The box will close at the back by means of a drop panel or a trap.

to the cage wire with its neck feathers lightly spread out as an invitation for scratching.

The second step: This is more difficult for now your parrot has to get used to getting onto your hand. Quietly hold one hand out to it and with the other offer it a treat, that you slowly pull back so that the bird is forced to put one foot on the outstretched hand. Only with endless patience and regular repetition will this finally succeed in moving the parrot to climb onto the extended hand. Stay calm and avoid doing anything that might frighten the Amazon. Even if it pecks your hand or tries to bite you, be patient and constantly bear in mind that you can't train a parrot like a dog. Punishment in any form is meaningless and destroys the carefully built-up relationship of trust.

The Tame Parrot

In time, Amazons come to think of themselves as full-fledged members of the family with all the rights but none of the obligations this entails. They also learn to assert their rights. When they feel they are not getting enough attention, many parrots demand their keeper's notice by whistling or producing other sounds, rattling their food dishes, or screeching nonstop. You obviously cannot always give in to a parrot's wishes for admiration and entertainment; still, you should not neglect a single bird too much or it might become a screamer or start pulling out its feathers.

Most tame Amazons are friendly only toward the people they know well. Even birds that are quite used to life in captivity and have been part of the family for years still regard strangers with great suspicion. When there is an unfamiliar guest in the house, they retreat to the farthest corner of the cage and act with reserve even toward their caretaker. It is impossible to get them to say any of the phrases, whistle any tunes, or mimic other sounds they ordinarily regale you with all day long. This is especially true if you have bragged about your parrot's amazing repertoire and have promised your guests a performance. Don't let the parrot's stubbornness upset you, and don't try to punish it by ignoring it. Parrots seldom behave according to your wishes.

How Amazons Learn to "Speak"

It's time to think of "speech training" only when the Amazon has largely gotten over its shyness. Because the bird is at its most receptive in the evening hours, the training should be done every evening. Parrots learn most quickly words that contain many vowels (a, e, i, o, u). The training program thus begins with words like Mama, Papa, good-bye, or hello. Sibilants are the hardest sounds for a parrot to learn. Through frequent talking in front of it and regular repetition, almost every Amazon will learn some words. Some parrots—depending on disposition and capability—develop into regular "performers" that can repeat whole sentences or many words; others are talented whistlers, whistling melodies, even in different pitches. Still others are able to reproduce sounds that they frequently hear in their environment.

The mimicking of Amazons—in contrast to the performance of an African Gray parrot—usually sounds quite parrotlike, in part even meaningless, and many times only suggesting the tone in which one has spoken words or

An example of a large outdoor aviary.

sentences to it or tones that they have heard most frequently.

Please do not expect too much of your Amazon; not every Amazon is a "performer," but almost every one does, with proper care and maintenance, develop into a lovable, devoted house pet.

Why Parrots Can "Speak"

Parrots belong to the mockers in the bird world, that is, to those birds that are able to imitate sounds. Among them only parrots have developed the ability to a true mastery. Still, every "speech utterance" of a parrot is merely a mechanical repetition; it doesn't understand the meaning of its words. Of course, many parrots can connect certain circumstances meaningfully with one another and so it often has the appearance of repeating some words with understanding and at the right moment.

When you want to teach a parrot "speech" or imitation, you develop and use its natural ability, but this is not behavior that could hitherto have been established in nature, although it is assumed that parrots imitated sounds frequently heard there, such as the "voices" of other animals.

Play and Activities

Singly kept parrots need regular activity to make their solitude bearable. Parrots that live in aviaries are less subject to the danger that they will vegetate and pine away from boredom because they have roomier living quarters, branching perches, and climbing trees, as well as companions and brooding activities. On the other hand, this danger is a constant one for the single parrot. If an Amazon is left alone too much, if it has neither a companion nor a human substitute partner around it regularly, changes occur in the bird. At first the Amazon becomes completely quiet, sits all day, hour after hour, in the same spot on its perch, and leaves it only occasionally for feeding. Frequently, such poor creatures turn to constant screeching and pulling out their feathers; some even begin to mutilate themselves (see Feather Eating, Feather Picking, page 48). You must avoid the possibility of these negative developments by providing varied activities or, even better, by getting your Amazon a partner.

"Playthings" for Amazons

Offer your Amazon variety and occupation by furnishing the bird cage—and, of course, the aviary and the flight cages, too—with large-linked chains and ropes for gnawing and climbing, with fresh branches, and with "toys" made of unprinted cardboard or wood dangling on chains. There are almost no limits on your inventiveness. The more varied the opportunities for activity are, the better. It's important to use material that isn't harmful to the bird or can't be bitten, such as some plastic toys, and swallowed. But remember, providing all these chances for activity doesn't exempt you from the attention that you must give your single Amazon daily and in sufficient quantity.

Flying Free in the House

Free flight inside the house is necessary for two reasons: first, to provide the bird with some change, and second, to offer it adequate opportunities for exercise. As soon as your parrot has gotten over its shyness, you should open the cage door and accustom it for an

hour at a time to being outside the cage. It's best if you place the bird on a climbing tree. If you furnish it with some fresh branches, the Amazon will soon adopt it as its favorite place and will lose interest in such landing spots as lampshades or cupboard edges.

Let the parrot fly and climb around the room only under supervision, since it can injure itself in some situations (see Dangers for Your Amazon, pages 30-31) or else can damage the furniture with its sharp beak. The parrot should always find its food in the cage, then it will quickly learn to clamber back there when it gets hungry. It should always spend the night in the cage.

The Hispaniolan Amazon (**Amazona ventralis**) *in an outdoor aviary.*

Dangers for Your Amazon

Source of Danger	Consequences	How to Avoid
Bathroom	Flying out of an open window. Drowning by falling into open toilet or filled sink or tub. Poisoning by cleaning materials, and so on.	Keep parrots out of the bathroom; never leave the bathroom door open.
Electric wires	Shock from gnawing or biting through wires.	Conceal wires under moldings and carpets, behind cupboards, or unplug.
Poisons	Severe disturbances (gastrointestinal, neural, and so on) by tin, copper, nicotine, mercury, plastic-coated bowls, cleaning materials, and insecticides; harmful are pencil lead, ballpoint and felt-tip pens, alcohol, coffee, spices.	Remove any and all poisonous materials from the bird's surroundings, or at least prevent it from getting at them. Be especially careful about lead curtain weights— parrots love to gnaw on them.
Poisonous trees, bushes, houseplants	Severe disturbances, often fatal.	Don't give bird any branches of poisonous trees or bushes to chew on. For example, the following are poisonous: acacia, birch, yew, laburnum, viburnun, holly, dwarf elder, and all conifers. Keep the parrots from nibbling or eating houseplants.
Plate glass	Flying into it, resulting in concussion or broken neck.	Cover glass on windows, balcony doors, glass walls, and so on, with curtains or get the parrot used to what seems to be an invisible room boundary: lower shades to two-thirds; increase the uncovered surface a bit each day. Place decals on the glass doors so the bird knows the doors are there.

Dangers for Your Amazon (continued)

Source of Danger	Consequences	How to Avoid
Adhesives	Poisoning with fatal outcome caused by volatile solvents.	Remove all animals from the room while using adhesives and air the room very thoroughly after work is finished.
Kitchen	Steam and fumes burden the respiratory passages; overheated kitchens and necessary ventilation lead to colds and other illnesses. Burns from stove burners, turned off but still hot, and from hot food in open containers.	Don't keep birds in the kitchen or else air it regularly; be careful; however, that there are no drafts. Place pots of water on hot burners that are not in use; cover pots.
Doors	Caught or crushed in carelessly closed or opened door. Birds may also fly away.	Accidents and escape can be avoided only with the greatest vigilance.
Cigarettes	Smoky air is injurious; nicotine is fatal.	It's best to not smoke in the vicinity of the bird, but at least ventilate regularly (avoid drafts).
Drafts	Colds, lung inflammations.	Avoid drafts no matter what. Also, avoid exposure to a direct flow of cold air from an air conditioner. If the entire house is air-conditioned, deflect the flow of air away from the bird's cage.

The St. Vincent Amazon (Amazona guildingii).

Two Amazons that get along well together. Left, a Red-lored Amazon (Amazona autumnalis salvini); *right, an Orange-winged Amazon* (Amazona amazonica).

The Amazon

The "Shower Bath"

A weekly shower helps parrots to keep their plumage in order.

In the house, parrots are best showered with a hand-held water sprayer. Use only lukewarm water and provide a gentle water stream with a fine mist and not a stream of water. All parrots are leery of such showering at the beginning; therefore, you must get them used to it slowly and carefully until they are comfortable with the weekly showering procedure.

Warning: Do not use a mister/sprayer that has previously contained household cleaning solutions.

In the flight cage, in summer, a warm rain shower can take the place of the shower, or the inmates can be sprayed weekly with a hose to which a fine spray head has been attached.

The showering time should be morning, preferably, so that the parrots are stimulated to a careful preening of the damp feathers and can be dry again before dark.

All parrots learn to enjoy the weekly shower; some birds may even enjoy it daily.

Cutting Claws

Rough perching branches of different sizes normally hamper the overgrowth of claws; however, should the claws become too long, they must be cut. You can hold a tame parrot in your hand for this, grasping its toes between two fingers. A parrot that is not tame must be caught—wear leather gloves—and held firmly with both hands, while a helper cuts the claws.

Using a sharp pair of nail clippers, cut the claws to normal length (see drawing, page 35). Be careful not to injure the blood vessel. In Amazon species that have bright, horn-colored claws, it's easy to see the blood vessel if you hold the claw against a bright light source. In Amazons with dark claws, claw cutting should be undertaken only with extreme caution.

If, in spite of all care, bleeding occurs because the claws were cut too short, put the bird back in the cage and let it stay there completely undisturbed for a while. The bleeding will usually come to a stop by itself; if this is not the case, call a veterinarian for advice.

Important note: Inexperienced parrot keepers should have the claw cutting done by an avian veterinarian or an experienced aviculturist.

Shortening the Beak

Abnormally long beak growth and particularly the occasional deformities that occur in the beak area (such as "crooked bite") are not always caused by lack of opportunity to wear it down; sometimes the cause is a metabolic disturbance resulting from inadequate diet. You should never, under any cir-

During a shower bath, the parrot will turn and bend, and spread his wings wide so as to wet all his feathers.

cumstances, undertake correction of beak abnormalities yourself, but always leave them to an experienced veterinarian or aviculturist.

The Cage

A parrot cage must be cleaned regularly, as a dirty cage can cause disease. The following cleaning procedures are necessary.

Daily: Clean food and water dishes, refill, empty spoiled food remains out of the floor tray.

Weekly: Empty the dropping tray and clean, dry, and spread the floor with a thin layer of clean sand. Use clean beach sand or the "bird sand" you can buy in a pet store, which has the advantage of an anise additive, that helps to keep down the odors around the bird cage.

Caution: Do not spread the cage floor with newspaper or, especially, aluminum foil; it's dangerous for the parrot if it eats any of it, and besides, it then can't eat the stones that foster digestion (see page 00), which are contained in sand.

Every six months: In galvanized or chrome-plated cages, scrub the perches and the cage mesh thoroughly under hot running water. Wash brass cages with lukewarm water and dry with a towel.

As necessary: Replace plastic dishes with new ones, since they become unsightly with time and then can no longer be thoroughly cleaned.

Cleaning of the Aviary and Flight Cage

Daily: Clean food and water dishes, refill, and remove spoiled food remains.

Weekly (or every two weeks): Rake out the floor of the cage and, whenever necessary, spread with clean sand.

Yearly: General cleaning is best done in the fall, after the breeding season. With the help

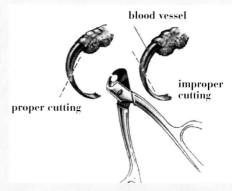

Cutting claws: On the left, correctly done; on the right, incorrectly done. Be careful not to injure the blood vessel!

of a garden hose and a scrub brush, clean the bird shelter and the cage thoroughly and afterwards disinfect it; replace the perches and renew the sand on the floor.

Important: All parrots must be removed to another place during the cleaning and may only be returned to the aviary when it is dry, the remains of the disinfectant have dried away, and the cage floor has been spread with new sand.

A tip on wing clipping: Trim the secondaries and the inner primaries (the white part of the feathers) on both wings. Never clip only one wing—the Amazon would lose its balance when trying to take off and fall to the ground.

PROPER DIET

According to existing information from the wild, Amazons are unspecialized seed and fruit eaters, and therefore in captivity they quickly get used to a substitute feed.

The Basic Diet

The parrot feed offered in the pet stores, in combination with the additional supplements discussed below, is generally regarded as suitable for Amazons. It consists of 40 to 50 percent white, striped and/or black sunflower seeds, with the other 50 to 60 percent divided among equal parts of peanuts, corn, oats, wheat, rice, millet, and canary grass seed, or white seed and thistle. Pine tree seeds and pumpkin seeds are sometimes also ingredients in this mixture. However, there are some doubts as to whether the high fat content of the sunflower seeds (54 percent), which often make up the major portion of the mixture, is particularly beneficial to the digestive tract of the Amazon; furthermore, sunflower seeds are very addictive due to their sweet taste and lack lysine, which is important for feather growth. Therefore, we assemble the feed mixture for our parrots ourselves; you can get all the ingredients at the pet store or from a feed dealer or buy one of the better-known commercial brands. The proportions of the mixture are about 30 percent sunflower seeds, 35 percent thistle, as well as

Two Yellow-crowned Amazons (Amazona ocrocephala) indulge in a snack.

35 percent of other seeds like millet, sorghum, rice, wild rice, buckwheat, white seed, and oats. Acorns, hazelnuts, walnuts, and pine nuts are considered treats by many Amazons but, all the same, we give our Amazons only very small amounts of them. On the other hand, most Amazons relish millet spray.

Sprouted Feed

Seed sprouts are enjoyed by many Amazons—once they get used to it. This sprouted feed is important for a healthy diet for Amazons, especially in winter when there is no green food and fruit is expensive, but also shortly before and during reproduction. In the stores there are contrivances—so-called sprouting boxes—that make the production of sprouts much easier. Appropriate seeds are oats, wheat, and also small seeds, such as those sold for small parakeets, canaries, and waxbills. All

Sunflower seeds tend to be an Amazon favorite, but be careful not to offer too many.

seeds are separated from one another and sprouted and then combined in one dish at feeding. Also welcome is a mixture of soaked or sprouted sunflower and/or safflower seeds, boiled corn, sprouted mung beans, and boiled peanut kernels mixed in one container.

The simplest method for production of sprouted feed is to put two days' supply of seed in a dish, cover the seeds with water, and place in a warm spot. After 24 hours shake the seeds, which will have swollen, in a fine-meshed sieve and wash them thoroughly under running water. Then spread the seeds on flat wire racks, keep them warm, and during the next 24 hours rinse them thoroughly several times. After two or three days, depending on the action of the warmth, the sprouts will have broken through on the oats and wheat. Wash again and offer to the parrots in a separate

dish. Give the parrots only as much as they can eat in a few hours.

Important: In summer the dish must be removed after a few hours and cleaned, because sprouted feed rots quickly in warm temperatures.

Fruit and Green Feed

In the wild, parrots gain a large part of their nutritional requirements by eating various kinds of fruit and fresh greenery. Appropriate food—that is, fruit and greenery—should also be included in the diet of a parrot in captivity.

Fruit: After becoming acclimated, parrots eat everything that the store or your own garden has to offer: apples, pears, plums, cherries, grapes, also exotic fruits such as oranges, bananas, mangos, papayas, kiwis, and whatever other fruit there is. Added to that are carrots, cucumbers, pieces of pumpkin and zucchini, berries of all kinds—strawberries, cranberries, blueberries, gooseberries, red currants—as well as the red fruits of the mountain ash and the hips of the dog rose (curs. Rosa canina).

Green feed: The palette of suitable green feeds ranges from garden vegetables such as lettuce, spinach, white beet, and dandelion leaves to countless wild plants such as shepherd's purse and chickweed.

Suitable food plants. Left, dandelion; right, flower stem and a whole plant of shepherd's purse; above right, chickweed.

Important: If you want to collect wild plants yourself, learn about them in the literature (see Information, page 84). Collect only those plants that you can identify without any doubt.

Caution: Chickweed is easy to confuse with the poisonous spurge. Definite identifying characteristic: If you break the stem of spurge, it exudes a milky fluid, whereas chickweed does not.

Animal Feed

Although parrots prefer to eat plants and their seeds and fruits, they also need animal protein. This need can be met with small portions of hard-boiled egg, cottage cheese, cheese, or canned dog food, given regularly, at ten-day intervals.

Pellets

Most bird food manufacturers now offer pelleted food designed specifically for a particular species of bird. These provide balanced nutrition and much less mess and waste. Unfortunately, parrots that are already eating seed may not make an easy transition to pellets. A good technique is to offer both seeds *and* pellets and try crumbling the pellets onto fruits or vegetables. *Never* try to starve a parrot until it gives in and eats the pellets.

Inappropriate Food for Parrots

Strongly seasoned food from the family table is very unhealthy for parrots. Even if your Amazon begs and is agitating for a slice of sausage or casts sidelong glances at a mouthful of stew, such things do not belong in the parrot's diet.

Table Scraps

Amazons enjoy a wide variety of table scraps: cooked vegetables, pasta, rice, brown bread, cake, toast, cheese, yogurt, and, in moderation, an occasional (unsalted) potato chip.

Breeding Food

Circumstances permitting, you should give an Amazon pair that is ready to breed a special breeding food (see Breeding Amazons, page 53). The pair will already be used to the food before the birth of the young, so there will be no slowdown in the food supply after the babies are born.

The breeding food is made of an egg mixture, available from the pet store, for example CéDé, and grated carrots; the mixture should be damp and crumbly. As necessary, parrots can also be given vitamins, calcium, fruit, and small pieces of cut-up egg, and greenery. To accustom the Amazons quickly to the unusual but very nutritious feed, offer it many times in succession.

Vitamins and Minerals

The diet described is complete and sufficient; however, in winter, when there is little fruit and little greenery around to feed, or after vacation, when the substitute caretaker has fed the parrot with only the basics, we recommend adding a multivitamin preparation to the drinking water, to avoid the development of any deficiencies; for dosage and application, follow the manufacturer's instructions.

The Orange-winged Amazon (**Amazona amazonica**) *is a rather small species and makes a pleasant pet.*

The Blue-cheeked Amazon (**Amazona dufresniana**) *is considered to be rather rare in Surinam.*

Amazons can get the necessary minerals with calcium available from the pet store, which you sprinkle over fruit and sprouts or mix in with the breeding food weekly. In addition, Amazons need mineral blocks, cuttlebone, and grit, as sold for racing pigeons; this also serves to supply their mineral requirements, and the grinding function assists the gizzard. These food additives are necessary for life; if they are lacking for a long period of time, the parrot can die because it can't digest its food properly. Therefore, you should always use sand on the bottom of the cage and offer grit in a separate dish.

Drinking Water

Amazons need fresh tap water daily. In districts with poor-quality drinking water, treat the water with a filter or use spring water, available in gallon containers at your grocery store.

Don't put the water dish near the food dish; almost all Amazons are very wasteful of their food and spread it around the whole cage. The food remnants will then dirty the water even sooner than usual.

Proper Feeding

To permit proper feeding of the parrot in calibrated amounts, the cage should contain three dishes: one dish each for mixed seeds and/or pellets, one for clean drinking water, and one for finely chopped green feed, fruit, sprouts (alternating), or, when necessary, rearing food. Be sure that the dishes are always clean, and give each parrot or pair the same dishes in the usual arrangement.

Feeding time: Always feed at the same time, either in the morning or the afternoon. We always feed our Amazons between 4:00 and 5:00 P.M., a bit earlier in winter. They are very active at this time and, furthermore, they can ingest enough food before nightfall.

Quantities: The food you put out should always consist half of dried seeds and half of green feed, fruit, and sprouts. Before and during the breeding period, the portion of sprouted seed can be increased and the ordinary diet can be enriched with breeding food. The daily amount is determined by the activity of the parrot. Caged birds, which move little, need about 2.8 ounces (80 grams) of seeds per day and about the same quantity of fruit. This is in accordance with the size of the feed dish that is usually supplied with the commercially available parrot cage.

Amazons kept in a small inside aviary in winter need, per pair and day, about 6.3 ounces (180 grams) of seed and the same amount of fruit. During the flight-cage season—the warm season—this quantity increases to about 8.75 ounces (250 grams) of seed and the same amount of fruit, and for reproduction, many times more.

A Sample Daily Diet for Your Amazon

Seed Mixture—½ ounce (15 g) per day per parrot:

Barley 5%	Hemp 5%	Sorghum 5%
Buckwheat 5%	Melaleuca seed 5%	Sunflower/safflower 15%
Canary grass seed 10%	Millet 5%	Wheat 10%
Corn 15%	Oats 5%	
Eucalyptus seed 5%	Paddy 10%	

Nuts—½ to ¾ ounce (15–20 g) per day per parrot; in separate dish; a mixture of the following possibilities:

Almonds	Grated Coconut	PeanutsWalnuts
Brazil nuts	Macadamia	Pine nuts

Tip: Place one drop of wheat germ oil in the open end of a peanut during breeding season.

Fruits—1½ ounces (40 g) per day per parrot; a choice of:

Apple (cut in pieces or quarters)	Fresh Figs	Pandamus serew pine
Banana (cut in pieces)	Grapes	Papaya
Berries (elder, mountain, ash, pyracantha)	Grapefruit	Pineapple
	Guava	Plums
Cherries	Mulberries	Pyracantha
Eugenia	Orange (cut in pieces)	Tomato

Greens—¾ ounce (20 g) per day per parrot; a choice of:

Acacia blossoms	Dandelion	Spinach
Calendula buds	Dock	Squash
Carrot tops and strips	Lantana blossoms	Twigs of Willow, Ash,
Celery	Lettuce	Hawthorn, Acacia, and
Chickweed	New Zealand spinach	fruit trees (NO cherry!)
Comfrey or hydroponically sprouted (7–8 days) barley, oats, or wheat	Shepherd's purse	Watercress
	Sow Thistle and other varieties	Zucchini

Vegetables—½ ounce (15 g) per day per parrot; a choice of:

Carrots	Fresh corn on the cob
Green beans and peas in the pod	Sweet potatoes

Extras—free-choice

Cooked beans and pulse; boiled corn	Cubes of hard cheese
Cooked chicken on the bone	Cuttlebone (available at all times)
Crumbled, dried chicken eggshell	Dry or semisweet biscuits

HEALTH AND ILLNESS

With proper maintenance and good care Amazons seldom become sick, as a rule. But even an experienced parrot keeper can occasionally make a mistake in care, producing conditions in which sicknesses occur or are fostered. Moreover, it does happen that for some reason parrots suffer a reduction in their natural resistance, without the keeper being able to see why or to do anything about it, and this may also result in illness.

Common Illnesses

The illnesses described below are frequently caused by mistakes or neglect in care and maintenance or are at least promoted by them.

Infestation with Ectoparasites (External Parasites)

Parrots can be attacked by mites *(Acarus)*, feather mites, or lice. The parasites live on the body surface and in the plumage of the infested bird. In well-kept parrots, the infestation is seldom very great.

Symptoms: The infested bird is restless, preens itself often and extensively, and scratches itself frequently with its toes and claws because it is constantly irritated by itching. Bald spots appear on the head, belly, and under the wings by degrees.

The Red-necked Amazon (**Amazona arausiaca**).

Possible causes: Frequent neglect of cleaning procedures; other causes are possible—ask the veterinarian.

Treatment: Dust the bird sparingly with an appropriate insecticide containing pyrethrin or cabaryl (ask advice of the pet dealer or veterinarian) and treat the whole cage.

Caution: To avoid poisoning, pay strict attention to the following points:
✔ Only use an insecticide on which the manufacturer has specifically stated that it is suitable for use on caged birds.
✔ When dusting the bird, protect the eyes, nose, and beak with your hand.
✔ Never treat a bird with spray.
✔ When you are treating the cage, always take the bird out of it.

Prevention: Regular, thorough cleansing of the cage during which all the wooden parts are scrubbed with hot water containing Lysol (4 ounces per gallon of water) or one-stroke Environ ($\frac{1}{2}$ ounce per gallon of water).

Infestation with Endoparasites (Internal Parasites)

Parrots are primarily attacked by tapeworms (Cestoda), mawworms (Ascaridia), and hair- or threadworms (Capillaria).

Symptoms: There are no typical manifestations of illness; the ailing bird often sits with ruffled feathers, slowly loses weight, and excretes slimy, thin, and usually foul-smelling stools. Sudden death can occur as the result of an intestinal blockage caused by hundreds of worms, usually mawworms.

Possible causes: Unhygienic maintenance promotes the illness.

Immediate measures: Fecal examination at the first signs of the illness; early treatment can lessen the extent and consequences of worm infestations.

Treatment: By the avian veterinarian. Only he or she can prescribe the proper medication (Dimetridazole, Metronidazole, Levamisole, Yomesan, or Piperazine); the directions for use should be followed exactly. An overdose can be dangerous for the parrot.

Prevention: Regularly clean bird cages thoroughly. Have the droppings of parrots that live in a flight cage examined for worms a number of times during the year.

Intestinal Inflammation (Enteritis)

This is one of the most frequent health problems with parrots.

Symptoms: General manifestations of illness (see page 50) are diarrhea, increased water intake, as a consequence of the need to replace lost fluids, and decreased appetite, so that this illness can signify a serious, sometimes life-threatening risk for the parrot.

Note: Psychological factors can induce a diarrhea-like stool, which is not to be considered a consequence of an intestinal inflammation. Thus, for example, the sight of a predator hanging in the air or of a cat lurking on the aviary roof, anxiety at being caught by the keeper or at being attacked by a rival parrot can lead to a sudden, watery diarrhea.

Possible causes: Spoiled feed, changed diet, ingestion of poisonous materials, such as lead, lead weights in curtains, enamel, cleaning materials, colds, parasite infestation, bacterial infections *(Escherichia coli [E. coli]* and *Salmonella)* fungi, and viruses.

Immediate measures: Offer chamomile tea and soft food, and infrared therapy (see page 50). If the bird seems very feeble or if the first aid measures don't lead to improvement within a few hours, take a fecal sample and go to the veterinarian at once.

Treatment: A treatment by medication must be ordered by the veterinarian. Follow his or her advice exactly.

Prevention: Avoid causes and institute treatment early.

Salmonellosis (Paratyphoid Infection)

Food or water contaminated with salmonellae causes salmonellosis. The disease can also be transmitted by such carriers as wild birds, especially city pigeons, rats, mice, and flies that live in or near the aviaries and introduce pathogens in their droppings.

Symptoms: There are no characteristic symptoms beyond the general ones. Only a laboratory analysis of the droppings can show whether salmonellae are present.

Treatment: Give a broad-spectrum antibiotic such as nitrofurazone or furazolidone, but only on the advice of an avian veterinarian and in accordance with directions.

Reminder: Because salmonellosis can be transmitted to humans, take proper precautions when handling sick birds.

Trichomoniasis

This is an infection caused by a microscopic protozoan called a trichomonad. The infection is hardly ever acute in mature parrots, but it can be passed on to, and take on active form in, nestlings fed from the parent's crop.

Symptoms: In the acute form of this disease, a thick yellowish coating covers the mucous membranes of the mouth and crop, interfering with food intake and even with breathing.

Treatment: The avian veterinarian can give you effective medications such as dimetridazole for both prevention and treatment.

Crop Inflammation

The ingestion of dirty water, spoiled or unsuitable food, or anything not meant to be eaten can lead to an inflammation of the mucous membranes in the crop. The inflammation may be caused by poisonous substances or by fermentation in the crop, as well as by pathogens such as bacteria, fungi, or trichomonads that are often present in healthy birds but that can cause inflammation if general resistance is lowered.

Symptoms: In addition to the usual general signs of illness, you may observe loss of appetite and vomiting of a viscid, brownish white slime that gradually turns the plumage of the head dirty and sticky.

Treatment: Consult the veterinarian for effective treatment and medication. Administer Maalox or DiGel to soothe the crop and neutralize the acid.

Aspergillosis

Aspergillosis is an infection caused by molds and affects primarily young birds and those weakened by age. It attacks the respiratory system because the pathogen is normally inhaled.

Symptoms: The major symptom is abnormal breathing, which does not, however, become apparent until the disease has reached an advanced stage.

Prevention: Keep the birds under optimal conditions. Poor hygiene, mass conditions, spoiled food, heat, and moisture all foster the growth and spreading of mold. Breeders should be especially careful during the mating season to provide the right kind of litter in the nest boxes. Although some breeders favor damp peat moss as litter, we do not recommend it because aspergillus flourishes in it. More suitable are excelsior and sawdust from coniferous trees, both of which discourage the growth of the mold.

Treatment: The mortality rate of birds with aspergillosis is high. Treatment is complicated and expensive and requires care by a veterinarian who is knowledgeable about bird diseases.

Coccidiosis

Coccidia are one-celled parasites that live in the mucous membranes of the intestinal tract of the parrot.

Symptoms: Coccidia can cause severe inflammation of the mucous membrane, result in intestinal bleeding, with accompanying manifestations of diarrhea and weight loss.

Possible Causes: Unclean housing conditions and bad health promote the illness.

Treatment: Only the veterinarian can prescribe appropriate medication, such as sulfa drugs.

Prevention: Regular, thorough cleaning and disinfecting of the cage area and fecal examination; this is important because if treatment is begun early, the bird can be free of the coccidia after a short time.

Respiratory Ailments

Disturbances of the respiratory tract can arise from very different causes. A diagnosis

Feather picking. A singly kept parrot is most likely to become a feather picker. The best remedy is to provide a companion.

Feather Eating, Feather Picking

This is an uncommon manifestation, which probably belongs to the psychological illnesses. Most often affected are singly kept parrots.

Symptoms: Extension of occasional plucking out and biting of single top feathers, especially in the shoulder or breast area, to the complete balding of the body, with the exception of the unreachable head feathers. There have even been recorded cases of self-mutilation, in which the skin or the musculature beneath it are gnawed.

Possible causes: Inadequately understood, yet until more is determined, it is possible to surmise that the coinciding of some of the following factors produces feather eating or picking, or at least promotes it:

✔ Not enough chance to exercise, such as being kept in a narrow cage.

✔ Boredom in "sterile quarters."

✔ Frustration or unhappiness over a major change in the parrot's surroundings or lifestyle.

✔ Continued stress in close quarters with other birds in one cage or a group in an aviary.

✔ Missing or wishing for a companion, especially with singly kept parrots.

✔ Missing a sexual partner at the onset of maturity, especially among aviary and breeding birds.

✔ Skin diseases that cause itching.

✔ Inadequate diet, incorrect environmental temperature, inadequate humidity.

✔ Lacking opportunities for bathing or lacking regular showers.

is difficult at best and often is impossible in a living bird.

Symptoms: General manifestations of illness (see page 50), repeated sneezing, damp or stuffed-up nostrils, discharge from the nose, labored breathing where the bird sits with legs spread and breathes with open beak and the tail moves up and down with every breath, noisy breathing; usually conjunctivitis of the eyelid also occurs.

Possible causes: Attack on the respiratory tract by bacteria, viruses, or fungi; cold from a draft or wrong or suddenly changed maintenance temperature; other causes are also possible.

Immediate measures: Infrared therapy (see page 50). If there is no improvement after 12 hours, the parrot needs veterinary help. With obvious breathing difficulty and noisy breathing, go to the avian veterinarian at once.

Treatment: Only by the veterinarian. Early treatment can increase the prospect of healing. Successful treatment is not possible in every case.

The Yellow-faced Amazon (**Amazona xanthops**).

Treatment: If your bird begins to pluck its feathers, try to think back and reverse any changes that you may have made in its care, environment, or lifestyle. In some cases it is wise to move the affected parrot from a cage to a larger flight cage in which there is enough to keep it busy in the form of gnawing branches, chains, wooden playthings, rope ends, or climbing apparatus; if necessary, get a companion for the bird. Spend more time with your single parrot and make it "quality time." In our experience, the materials recommended by stores to prevent feather picking as a rule have no effect.

Prevention: Optimum maintenance conditions. For the singly kept parrot, give enough attention; better still, furnish it with a companion.

Parrot Fever (Psittacosis)

Parrot fever, or *psittacosis,* is by no means a common parrot disease. Therefore, we'll discuss it only briefly, because the name itself is known to lay people and it can produce serious, life-threatening manifestations in parrots as well as humans. Psittacosis is an infectious disease, which in fact does not affect only parrots. The causative agent of this disease has been detected in over 100 other bird species, in which case one speaks of ornithosis.

Symptoms: No characteristic symptoms. Sleepiness, weight loss, diarrhea, conjunctivitis of the eyelid, and decreased food intake can be accompanying signs of the illness.

Treatment: According to public health laws the disease must be reported and must be treated. Affected parrots are isolated according to the instructions of the public health officer and treated with an appropriate antibiotic.

Note: A psittacosis infection can become a life-threatening illness in human beings. Besides milder symptoms, something like those of a cold or flu, serious illnesses with high fever and infection of the respiratory tract have also been reported. The disease is curable if it is recognized in time and properly treated. Therefore, if you or a member of your family develop a severe respiratory disease advise your family doctor that you keep a parrot.

Precautions: Scarcely possible; it is important that a parrot be free of the pathogen when acquired; you will find further information about psittacosis in the specialists' literature and the newspapers (see Information, page 84). Be careful about buying parrots kept in large lots and under unhygienic conditions.

Common Signs of Sickness

There are some clearly recognizable signs that indicate a possible illness in a parrot. However, they seldom signal the exact kind of illness, since many ailments do not present an unequivocal picture. In any case, if you notice any symptom in your parrot, you should immediately consult a veterinarian who specializes in cage-bird illnesses.

A sick parrot has a continually ruffled plumage, rests frequently with head turned back, and exhibits no appetite. In many cases, additional symptoms appear, such as frequent sneezing, damp and sticky nostrils, changed feces, or cloudy eyes. As a rule, these symptoms indicate a general infection.

First-Aid Measures

Beginning parrot keepers should never try to treat their Amazons themselves; it's always true that the best first aid is a visit to the avian veterinarian at once.

Only a very experienced parrot keeper can possibly determine whether his or her Amazon is only slightly sick or whether the symptoms indicate a life-threatening illness.

In simple cases, the keeper can try to help the Amazon with infrared therapy.

Note: The veterinarian orders infrared or a similar heat therapy for many illnesses (80–85°F or 27–30°C). Therefore every Amazon keeper should know how to set it up.

Infrared or similar heat therapy: If several parrots are kept in the same flight cage, the sick bird must be separated from the others in the cage.

For infrared therapy, the parrot is placed in an ordinary parrot cage, which should stand in a separate, bright, quiet, heated room. The infrared or heat lamp should be placed at least 23½ inches (60 cm) from the cage and directed to cover only half the cage so that the parrot can seek out the temperature zone that is most comfortable for it or else can avoid the warmth.

Note: Pet stores sell special "hospital cages" for parrots, which can be warmed and lighted by heat lamps to different temperatures. Depending on your needs, the front consists either of plate glass or wire grating. The floor is a fine-mesh wire grate, which allows the droppings and the food remains to fall through

Infrared illumination is a healing treatment measure for many illnesses. The lamp should be directed only toward half the cage so that the parrot can go in and out of the heat.

so that they can't be stirred up, which is very important in avoiding some diseases.

Feeding: During the period of illness, unsweetened, lukewarm chamomile tea, Gatorade, honey, or corn syrup added to water (4 tbsp/qt) and soft, vitamin-rich food such as sprouted seed (see page 37), and the bird's favorite food should be offered; fruit and green feed should be omitted for the time being.

Caution: If the condition of the parrot does not improve within a few hours, a visit to the avian veterinarian is your only option.

The Visit to the Avian Veterinarian

If you can't get the name of a veterinarian who has experience with parrots from other parrot keepers or the pet store dealer, find out by telephone whether the veterinarian of your choice has adequate experience.

Transporting the bird to the veterinarian must be accomplished as quickly as possible. A transport box (see page 26) is most suitable; you should pad it with soft material; it is crucial to avoid bone-breaking and to protect the sick bird.

Important for the doctor is information about the care and feeding of the Amazon, the time of the appearance of the symptoms, and the course of the illness so far. It will be helpful if you've learned a little about bird illnesses ahead of time (see Common Illnesses, page 45, and the recommended literature on page 84).

It's best if you take a fecal sample with you that the veterinarian will usually examine

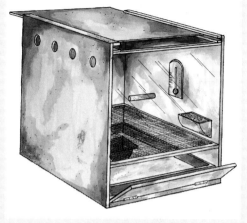

A basic hospital cage. Various designs are also commercially available.

right away. After diagnosis and treatment—often treatment by injection—the veterinarian will as a rule prescribe medication and advise care procedures for the ailing bird. If he or she does not suggest further care, ask whether infrared or heat therapy and soft food (see page 50) would be helpful for the sick Amazon.

The veterinarian will decide the length of the treatment. Follow his or her advice exactly, even if the Amazon obviously feels better and begins to jump around in its cage. Relapses are not uncommon when treatment is concluded too soon, and further treatment can then be very difficult.

BREEDING AMAZONS

The Washington Endangered Species Convention

Amazon parrots belong to the bird species that are threatened with extinction. All species are subject to the protection regulations of the Washington Endangered Species Agreement (called WC—Washington Convention—for short), an agreement to which more than 100 countries all over the world have become parties, among them the United States, England, the Netherlands, Australia, and Germany. The WC regulates the traffic in threatened animal and plant species in order to counteract their decline in nature. The threatened animal and plant species are listed in three appendices, according to the degree of endangerment; for each appendix there are special protection regulations. Nineteen of the 27 Amazon species are specified in Appendix I of the WC, which means that they are particularly endangered—traffic in them is forbidden. The other Amazon species are covered by the provisions of Appendix II.

Causes of the disappearance of the Amazons in their natural environment lie primarily in the destruction of their habitat. To gain lumber and arable land the forest districts of the habitat are being recklessly cleared. The brooding and food trees of the Amazon parrots are sacrificed to the power saw or uprooted by gigantic bulldozers.

The Panama Amazon (**Amazona ochrocephala panamensis**).

Breeding to Preserve the Species?

We are doubtless scarcely able to undertake anything effective against the destruction of the habitat of the Amazons, but the degree to which the Amazons become captive-bred lessens the number of the imported wild catch by that much. Fortunately the idea of species preservation has recently been attracting more and more attention from parrot fanciers as well as from pet dealers. It is thus agreed that breeding efforts must be intensified for preservation of the Amazon parrot species. Nevertheless, breeding for species preservation—particularly in the case of the Amazon parrot—is no simple matter; the following observations are in order:

✔ Amazon breeding is still in its infancy. Probabilities of success should not be equated with species protection programs. Reports of successful, consistent breeding attempts that might offer the possibilities of increase in the number of available birds are still very few. Nevertheless, attempts at breeding are being pursued methodically and will eventually certainly lead to success. Generally, the smaller and medium-sized Amazons, such as Cuba Amazon, blue-fronted Amazon, and yellow-fronted Amazon, are easier to breed than the larger species.

✔ Only when we succeed in breeding Amazons in noticeable numbers will we have taken the first step on the road to species protection.

✔ Perhaps at some point healthy captive-bred birds should be reestablished in their former distribution ranges to increase the diminished natural supply. In some cases, settlement in a substitute biotope will be necessary because of widespread habitat destruction. This challenge is fraught with many difficulties, which need not be discussed here. We hope that the foregoing information will stimulate as many parrot fanciers as possible to attempt breeding.

✔ The following instructions for methodical breeding preparations should help you, sooner or later, to be successful in your efforts to reproduce Amazons in captivity.

Legal Requirements for Amazon Breeding

There are no regulations for breeding Amazon parrots in the United States, Canada, or the United Kingdom. In Germany, Austria, Switzerland, and several other European countries, however, each parrot brood must be reported to the proper authorities. The breeder must file an application "for breeding and trade with parakeets and parrots." Before the application is validated, a federally appointed veterinarian will examine the applicant on his or her knowledge of breeding, and will check the purpose in breeding that you have entered on the aforementioned application. Breeders who receive permission are obligated to provide the young birds with official leg bands and must maintain a breeding record book. The details of origin, transfer, illnesses, treatment measures, and death of any of the parrots in question must be entered in this book. After permission has been granted, an inspection of the parrots by a federally appointed veterinarian will be undertaken at regular intervals.

We feel that this method should be adopted by all countries that embrace the Washington Convention.

Maintenance Conditions for Breeding

The following rules contain the most important requirements, which are determining factors for the success of breeding Amazons:

✔ You must succeed in putting together two mature, opposite-sexed Amazons of the same variety that are in harmony with each other.

✔ If possible house the two Amazons together in a separate outdoor aviary with a heated protected area (see page 22) and hang a suitable nest box in the inside room (see page 17). Be careful that the parrots don't keep destroying it.

✔ Pay attention to the relationship between maintenance temperature, molting, and reproductive cycles (see page 56).

✔ The feed must be measured and enriched during the breeding period.

The Breeding Pair

It doesn't work to set a male and female—the sexes should be definitely confirmed—in a single cage and then hope for offspring. The mutual "sympathy" of both parrots is vital for breeding success. If two Amazons do not get along together, they should be separated again after several weeks of trial. It is advantageous for the development of a pair if several Amazons of one species (or even subspecies) are available. A pair that develops this way will start out and live in a harmonious, lifelong partnership and will usually raise its young without any untoward incident.

Note: Even parrots of the same sex can form a harmonious "pair"; therefore, the sexes of the

Appropriate breeding sites: Left, a hollowed-out tree trunk (available in pet stores); its examination door is cut out of the side and closed with a metal pin. Right: A homemade nest box on which the roof and examination box can be raised.

breeding pair should be definitely confirmed (see page 11).

Housing and Nest Boxes

After partners are chosen it's advisable to give each pair a separate cage in which it will not be disturbed by its fellow birds. Otherwise, at the beginning of the mating period serious clashes can occur between rival Amazons, which can sometimes end in death.

Place the nest box in the inner room for protection from cold, wind, and dampness, if possible attached high under the roof. For all the Amazons described in this book, nest boxes with the following dimensions will be suitable: height, 31 to 39 inches (80–100 cm); inside diameter, 12 to 14 inches (30–35 cm); hole diameter, 4 to 5 inches (10–12 cm). (The white-fronted Amazons *(Amazona albifrons)* will also put up with smaller boxes.) You can find practical nest boxes in the pet shop. They have an opening in the lower portion through which you can see into the box to check on the young birds or to take out dead eggs. A layer of soft humus will allow for the proper positioning of the eggs under the weight of the brooding Amazon female.

Note: After the brooding period remove the nest box, clean it, disinfect it, repair if necessary, and let it dry until the beginning of the next breeding period.

Maintenance Temperature During Molting and Reproductive Cycles

In parrots there exists an important relationship between the maintenance temperature, the breeding cycle, and the molting season: As a rule, parrots do not breed during the molting period. The parrots must get used to a rhythm of life in which breeding can be completed at a time that is suited to our widely fluctuating climate (as in summer), and molting begun right afterward. This rhythm can be achieved by manipulating the maintenance conditions.

The following seasonal rhythm is necessary: In April/May, when it slowly becomes warmer in various parts of the United States, with the exception of Florida or California, where *year-round* breeding is possible, the courtship period must begin. Egg laying and brooding should take place in early summer; raising the young may last until the end of September. After that, molting must take place for four to eight weeks so that before the beginning of winter the parrots can replace the feathers that have become tattered during brooding with new

ones and, again completely and warmly protected, survive the winter well. This is how this
seasonal rhythm is achieved: In winter and
spring, from the beginning of November to the
beginning of April, the lodgings of the parrots
are only warmed to about 43 to 46°F (6–8°C).
The beginning of the warm season brings the
parrots into the breeding mood, and they begin
the business of mating. Molting then occurs—
as desired—in the fall. Though two years is the
average length of time it takes to adapt to
these conditions of seasonal rhythm favorable
for breeding, once established, the rhythm will
thenceforth be maintained.

Caution: Caged birds that are used to a
warm environment must slowly become used
to the lower maintenance temperatures
described above over the course of several
months.

Feeding of Breeding Birds

In the winter months parrots that are to be
bred receive the usual allotment of parrot food
(see Proper Feeding, page 42). Before the onset
of the breeding period, the food will be
enriched by the addition of stimulating nutri-
ent elements, such as sprouted seed or legumes
that have been soaked and then cooked, to
bring the birds to breeding pitch. At the same
time it is advisable to get the birds used to the
addition of a vitamin- and protein-rich nour-
ishing food that contains all the important
nutrients for the young as well as bread soaked
in water, or a whole wheat bread mixture. The
latter is very much appreciated by the author's
birds. To the whole wheat bread mixture I have
added a little raw egg, grated carrot, and
endive; this is then baked (see Breeding Food,
page 39).

Courtship and Mating

With the onset of the warmer weather,
sometimes as early as April but usually not until
early in May, Amazons begin courting. With
newly paired Amazons it can go along quite
conspicuously and at loud volume (for detailed
description of courtship behavior, see page 56).
Abundant social grooming, loud cries, and irres-
olute attempts by the male to feed the female—
called partner feeding, sometimes also called
courtship feeding—accompany the courtship,
which usually will last several days but sometimes lasts a few weeks. With older pairs, which
have already gone through breeding a number
of times, some elements of the breeding pattern disappear. In some instances, spontaneous
mating may even occur without any preliminary
wooing.

The courtship period comes to an end with
the first copulation. The matings, which sometimes last for many seconds, become increasingly frequent.

Egg Laying and Brooding

If the female remains squatting in the nest
hole for hours at a time and produces noticeably
large quantities of droppings, these are signs
that egg laying is imminent. In captivity, mostly
at the end of May or the beginning of June,
Amazon parrots lay two to four pure white eggs
on the humus covering of the nest box floor.

With the laying of the second egg, the
female begins her brooding, which, depending
on weather and brooding activity, may take
26 to 28 days. Mostly the female broods alone,
but sometimes the male squats beside the
female in the nest box or else visits the female
there to supply her with food.

Hatching and Rearing the Young

The young hatch at the same intervals as the eggs were laid. The female may provide help by picking at the eggshell. Newly hatched Amazons, like all altricial birds, are naked, barely fluffy, blind, and extremely helpless. They need between 70 to 100 days before they resemble the parents in size and weight, have developed a complete plumage, and are in a position to find their own food. In this period both parents have much to do with the feeding.

Feeding the Young

The male takes food from the feeding dishes and swallows it into his crop, where the first digestive process begins. He then feeds the predigested gruel-like food to his mate, who eventually regurgitates it—again predigested in the crop—and gives it to the young. In the first weeks of life, young parrots have a broadened, shovel-shaped lower mandible, into which the female puts the food, initially a thin fluid. Later, when the babies are older, the male also takes a direct part in the feeding.

During the feeding process, the feeding parent crosses its own beak with that of the young bird, regurgitates the food from its crop with pumping neck movements, and transfers it to the young bird with shaking, back-and-forth movements.

Problems During Incubation

Incubation does not always go smoothly and automatically result in baby birds. We have heard aviculturist friends say—and it has happened to us, too, more often than we would like—that "something went wrong" and the eggs did not hatch. Some possible reasons for failure are as follows:

Two Yellow-shouldered Amazons (**Amazona barbadensis**).

✔ Two newly matched parrots had not yet taken a liking to each other (and perhaps never will), so that no mating took place. In such situations, eggs are laid and conscientiously incubated by the female even though they are infertile. If this happens, the eggs should be removed after the normal incubation period. The female then often proceeds to lay a second clutch even if she belongs to a species that ordinarily raises only one brood per year.

✔ If the parent bird left the nest for too long, the eggs may have gotten too cold, causing the death of the embryos. The reason the bird may have left the eggs unattended is not always easy to determine, but one thing that is certain is that if the female is disturbed too often, she is likely to respond by leaving the nest.

✔ It happens not infrequently that fully developed parrot chicks die inside the egg shortly before hatching, usually because they are not

Egg tooth

This young bird is 15 days old, and the first quills are becoming visible on the wings.

Three young at the ages of 7, 9, and 10 days— their eyes are still closed; they usually open between the 15th and 26th day.

able to break out of the shell. The reason is that the air was too dry in the nest box, so that the shells became too hard and brittle for the fully mature chick to crack them. You can prevent this disappointing outcome by moistening the nesting material before the eggs are laid, and by spraying the outside of the nest box with water every so often during the incubation period. Of course, you should not overdo this by keeping the box constantly wet or dripping with water because, far from aiding the hatching process, the excess moisture may well kill the embryos.

Hand-feeding

It often happens that Amazon parrots—especially inexperienced first-time breeders—destroy eggs and kill newly hatched birds or leave the eggs because of frequent disturbances. In this last case you have the chance, if you recognize the situation in time, to bring the eggs along to further development in an incubator and to raise the hatched babies—or

An Amazon at the age of 26 days; the plumage on the wings, head, and tail can now be seen clearly.

the abandoned young birds—by hand. This possibility should be viewed only as a solution of necessity, because hand-raised young birds develop an attachment for humans in earliest infancy and are then very difficult to use later for breeding purposes. A committed parrot fancier will not resort to hand-raising merely to get tame, dependent young birds.

If the parents no longer visit the nest box and the danger arises that the young birds will die, the keeper must of course intervene and help.

Maintenance: Parrot chicks should be kept in a tank that is warmed to about 96.8°F (36°C); infrared lamps and the hospital cage described on page 50 serve very well.

Feeding and Food

In the beginning, the young parrots are provided with food about every two hours between 6:00 A.M. and 12:00 P.M. With newly hatched parrots the feeding is not begun until the second day. Powdered baby food is good feeding material. It is mixed with water and at two- to three-day intervals vitamin and mineral supple-

ments are mixed in. At feeding time the mixture must be at a temperature of 104 to 106°F (40–41°C). It must be mixed fresh daily.

As the birds get older, the intervals between feedings can be lengthened to about every three or four hours, the gruel can be thickened a bit with finely minced egg yolk, fruit, and vegetables, and its temperature lowered to lukewarm.

It is difficult to manage the crossover from gruel to solid seed feed. You should therefore accustom the young Amazon step by step to eating out of the feeding dish. In the beginning it should find its usual gruel there, then later soft fruit and greenery, and finally seeds as well. To teach the young bird how to remove the hulls from the seed, it's helpful if it can watch how another bird in a neighboring cage

Hand feeding. A young bird that has been abandoned by its parents can be fed by hand. The young bird is given the food gruel with a teaspoon.

This colorful Amazon is ready for high marks at an exhibition!

does this. Monitor the temperature of the environment; drafts and sudden temperature changes are injurious to young birds. Only when their plumage is complete can they be maintained at room temperature without additional sources of heat.

Hybrid Offspring

Hybrid offspring are the result of a successful mating between two birds of different species or races. As a rule, these matings are between members of the same genus (blue and gold and green-winged macaws, or blue-fronted and orange-winged Amazons) or between two races of the same species (yellow-cheeked and Lesson's Amazons). Successful matings between representatives of two different genera are much rarer and generally occur only if there is a close relationship between them. Examples are offspring from a hyacinth macaw (genus *Anodorphynchus*) and a blue and gold macaw (genus *Ara*) or from a lesser sulfur-crested cockatoo (genus *Cacatua*) and a rose-breasted cockatoo (genus *Eolophus*).

One recent example shows that even more distantly related parrots can produce viable offspring. In 1984 the crossing of a female Illiger's macaw and a male black-headed caique in the Duisberg Zoo (Germany) produced four healthy young parrots. Like most hybrids, they exhibited the shapes and markings of both parents.

In nature, matings between animals belonging to different species—and consequently the production of hybrid offspring—are prevented by various factors, such as nonsynchronous mating seasons, differences in courtship ritual, or geographic barriers, such as mountain ranges, that isolate different species from each other.

Still, hybrids or mongrels, as they are sometimes called, do occur in nature in areas where the ranges of two species meet and overlap. This phenomenon is scientifically documented, for instance in the border area between Brazil and Peru, where white-bellied and black-headed caiques occupy adjacent ranges and overlap because no river divides their territories. Hybrid parrots with characteristics of both species have been observed there. In the rest of these parrots' huge area of distribution, the Amazon River serves as a boundary that keeps the two species apart.

Frequency Among Captive Birds

Hybrid parrots turn up with some frequency among captive birds. When not enough or only unsatisfactory partners of the right species are available, birds of different species readily pair up, and the resulting relationship may be just as harmonious as that between a pair of similar birds. In many zoos where Amazons and macaws are kept together in large community aviaries, such "mixed marriages" are quite routine, although they do not always produce offspring. In the United States, crossings between different macaws, especially between the blue and gold *(Ara ararauna)* and the scarlet macaw *(A. macao),* are rather common, and the offspring are known as Catalina macaws.

Zoologists object on principle to the production of hybrids because, as has happened in many animal species in the past, it may hasten the extinction of some species in their original forms if the wild populations are already significantly decimated. It is true that hybrids generally cannot produce offspring of their own so that further change in the original gene composition is precluded, but there are a number of species in which the original form no longer survives—at least in our aviaries—because of human manipulation in attempts to breed birds for certain characteristics. Examples are the various Australian rosellas and red-fronted parakeets *(Cyanoramphus novaeze-landiae)* of New Zealand, whose different races have been arbitrarily crossed so often that probably not a single untampered specimen survives in captivity. A similar situation exists with African lovebirds. The masked, Fischer's, Nyasa, and black-cheeked lovebirds have been so manipulated and deformed by fanciers' breeding ambitions that it is often impossible to tell to which species or subspecies a particular bird should be assigned. All aviculturists should make it a point to get mates of the same species or race for their single parrots so that the birds can reproduce as they would in nature, namely, with birds of their own kind.

Bird Shows

In many places bird shows are held every year between September and December. Successful breeders can exhibit the young birds hatched in the course of the year and get a chance to compare them with those of other breeders. These events may be organized by local bird societies or groups of fanciers, by large regional or national groups, or by international organizations.

All the birds raised in captivity are presented in standard cages, organized by species and groups or color variants, to judges who compare the birds and evaluate them according to a number of criteria. The winning bird in each category—or rather the bird's owner—receives a trophy that will later serve as proof of the honor received at the exhibition.

Although by far the greatest number of exhibited birds are finches, canaries, rosellas, budgerigars (parakeets), and lovebirds, more and more parrots are shown, too, every year. We take this as a sign that breeding efforts with large parrots are becoming more frequent, which is presumably due at least in part to the ceaseless work and exchange of information in which the exhibiting groups and associations engage.

Should Parrots Be Exhibited?

If exhibiting one's birds becomes an end in itself and if, as we have seen among many aviculturists, the chase after trophies becomes the primary motive for breeding parrots, it is perhaps time to reexamine one's motives for having and breeding parrots.

It also seems questionable to us in general whether large parrots are suitable for exhibiting at all. After all, these parrots will probably never be bred on a sufficiently large scale for the criteria used in normal selective breeding of birds such as canaries and budgerigas to be applied. A veterinarian once defined "breeding," as the term is traditionally applied to domestic animals, as "the planned reproduction of an animal species, controlled by humans with the aim of stabilizing or enhancing certain characteristics or combining them in new ways to achieve specific goals in the next generation." This definition can be applied without hesitation to most of the birds seen at bird shows, but it is meaningless, and probably always will be, in connection with the large parrots discussed in this book. The idea of a show to compare one's own breeding results with those of others seems to me almost grotesque in connection with large parrots because at present we are not able to breed enough parrots to ensure the survival of all the species, let alone to start thinking of "selective" breeding for certain traits.

In our opinion there are other reasons as well for thinking twice before showing parrots at exhibitions.

Problems Connected with Exhibitions

Getting ready to go to a bird exhibition means the following for the parrots involved:
✔ Being torn out of their social community, which means temporary separation from other birds of the same species and especially from the mate.
✔ Having to get used to a small exhibition cage.
✔ Daily training to learn the proper sitting posture required by the exhibition guidelines.
✔ Washing and grooming of the plumage, involving repeated capture and handling of the birds.

When the date of the show arrives, this is what is in store for the parrots:
✔ A trip to the exhibition location.
✔ Adjustment to different temperatures from those to which the birds are accustomed at home.
✔ Bad air in the exhibition halls, often poisoned by cigarette smoke.

✔ The possibility of catching a disease from other birds, always a real danger even though the guidelines of many organizations require a veterinarian's certificate of health for all birds entering shows.
✔ Being disturbed continually by thousands of exhibition visitors, many of whom, from what we have seen, cannot refrain from trying to touch the birds through the bars or trying to get the bird's attention by rattling the cage.

It seems to us that any one of these points might dissuade a lover of parrots from getting involved in bird exhibitions. The cumulative impact of all these negative experiences on parrots seems to us cause for seriously questioning the concept and justification of these events and for reconsidering our own moral responsibility toward the birds in our care.

Whatever your feelings about bird shows may be, we urge you to visit one sometime and look at the parrots there with the eye of an objective observer. Perhaps you will understand what we mean when you see the plight of umbrella-crested and rose-crested cockatoos and even large macaws cramped into cages that are far too small to allow even the most basic of their occupants' needs.

To us, neither the chance to compare birds, which is meaningless, as we have already argued, nor the desire on the part of the exhibitor to have a larger audience appreciate a shelf of trophies justifies putting the birds through days of upheaval and discomfort.

UNDERSTANDING AMAZONS

How Amazons Live Together in Nature

By nature, Amazon parrots are very social birds. In their natural habitat they live together in groups and order their behavior in reference to the fellow Amazons.

The group size depends upon the food supply and the purpose of the grouping, for example, food-seeking, or sleeping companions. With the exception of the breeding season and in times of abundant plant and fruit growth, frequently gigantic swarms, which can include several hundred birds, are found together. Many times they go on searches for food together, often flying distances of many miles daily, to systematically harvest their favorite fruit or fruit parts from tree to tree. Some Amazons have developed into regular migrants, which change their location several times a year depending on the fruit harvest. Others are more or less permanently located but daily undertake extended flights to their feeding grounds.

Before dusk falls, the Amazons fly back to their roosting place for the night. Depending on the size of the group, they use one sleeping tree in common or several trees close together, into which they crowd and loudly defend their perches against one another.

Getting food can sometimes require acrobatic feats! Here, a Yellow-necked Amazon in her natural habitat.

Permanent pair bonding is entered into only with the onset of sexual maturity. Amazon pairs are usually easy to pick out during flight and at roosting because they stick closely together and there is much body contact. Young birds and subadult (not yet sexually mature) Amazons frequently group together in flocks of young birds, in which the pairs later meet. This pairing is not yet sexually motivated; it can be regarded as a kind of engagement period.

At the beginning of the breeding period, Amazons change their behavior in the group. They become increasingly aggressive toward their comrades, defend their sleeping places, and separate themselves more and more from the group. In a somewhat removed breeding area the pair occupies its own nesting hole and probably also territory, which they energetically defend against any intruder. For breeding holes Amazon parrots use abandoned woodpecker holes or rotted-out tree holes, which they widen with their strong beaks. The wood chips that fall on the hole floor, as well as the decayed wood that is already there, will not be removed from the nesting space but will serve as the proper medium for the eggs and to keep the required high humidity in the hole constant.

Egg laying follows courtship. Depending on the species, the female lays two to five eggs, which are incubated for 26 to 28 days.

Raising the young lasts for 10 to 14 weeks. When the young are independent, the small family band separates and the parents rejoin the other parrots in a group. The young birds remain in the vicinity of the parents for a while longer but become increasingly independent and sooner or later join together with parrots of the same age.

Important Behavior Patterns of Amazons

So far, unfortunately, we know very little about the behavior of the Amazon; scientific behavior studies still do not exist. To help Amazon keepers learn to understand their Amazon better and to stimulate them to make their own observations, we report on the most frequently noted behavior patterns of Amazons.

How Amazons Propel Themselves

Amazons love to climb; one gets the impression with those in cages and aviaries that climbing is the preferred way of movement for Amazon parrots. Still, you should not undervalue their flying capabilities and their need to fly, especially if you remember that many Amazons undertake long flights in the search for food. In roomy flight cages it is possible to observe that they make active, enthusiastic use of their wings. Many species, such as the white-fronted (A. albifrons), green-cheeked (A. viridigenalis), lilac-crowned (A. finschi), and orange-winged (A. amazonica) are very skillful fliers, while the blue-fronted (A. aestiva) and some varieties of the yellow-crowned Amazon fly clumsily ("helicopterlike"). In any case, Amazons have a great urge to fly. The parrot keeper must provide enough opportunities for exercise. Amazons go along the ground only reluctantly, and even on flat surfaces they move awkwardly with toes turned in pigeon-toed.

Feeding

Seeds are hulled in the beak with the help of the tongue, fruit and green feed minced with the beak. All the food is first stored in the crop and predigested before it is conveyed to the other digestive system for utilization.

Like almost all large parrots, the Amazon also uses its foot like a hand to grasp large pieces of food and to hold them to its beak for breaking into smaller pieces.

Amazons waste their food profligately, which every parrot keeper must learn to get used to; they nibble fruit and then leave it unnoticed; some root through the food bowl for favorite seeds and knock the less desirable kernels out of the dish with one "beak stroke."

Body Care

Amazons preen their feathers many times a day; the individual feathers are drawn through the beak and thus cleaned. The Amazon removes dirt and feather fragments from its beak by rubbing it on a hard surface, such as the perch. The toes are cleaned with the beak. To help with body care, the Amazon in captivity also needs a shower bath or a bathing tub filled with water (see The "Shower Bath," page 34, for information on bathing a parrot in your home).

Social Preening

The mutual scratching and preening of the feathers does two things for parrots: In the first place, head and undertail coverts, which the parrot cannot reach with its own beak, are

Preening: Amazons preen their feathers several times a day. In the process, each individual feather is cleaned by being pulled through the beak.

cleaned by the partner. Second, the social grooming has an important function in pairing and bonding. In conflict situations it is frequently observed that Amazons sit close together and mutually preen their feathers, obviously to reconfirm the partnership.

In critical situations, for example if a dog or an unknown human approaches, in which one would really expect a reaction such as flight or attack, they first scratch each other before they respond according to the situation.

Courtship Behavior

Besides social preening there is a whole list of other behavior patterns that are part of the courtship behavior of Amazons:

Display behavior: The Amazon male secures his breeding territory—even in an aviary—well in advance and protects it with striking behavior. On an exposed place in his territory, he struts, often screaming loudly, in an upright stance, with wings spread and tail feathers spreading open and closed. This has a terrifying effect on rival Amazons and also on birds of related parrot species. The impression is strengthened by optical signals provided by opening his wings and spreading his tail, displaying the extraordinary feather colors, which are in strong contrast to the usual mostly green color of the body plumage.

With time the aggressive mood of the male increases, and the display and threatening behavior is followed by a period of readiness to attack. Now fellow aviary inhabitants and even the keeper may become the victims of dangerous attacks, which not uncommonly conclude fatally for the fellow inhabitants of the aviary and often bloodily for the humans. During brooding, the male also secures the food supply against competition and protects the nest hole, female, and later the young birds from enemies.

The display behavior increases even more; besides opening the wings and spreading the tail, the neck and upper back feathers will also be spread from time to time. The male thus struts here and there, turning this way and that in order to be seen from all sides. In addition, from time to time he demonstrates his beak strength by biting off wood splinters from his climbing branches with powerful beak movements and throwing them to the ground.

If the chosen female appears, the male seems to try to intensify his efforts. Striking a

A White-fronted Amazon (Amazona albifrons) *with a piece of apple in its claw.*

Above: The Salvin's Amazon (Amazona autumnalis salvini) from Honduras to SW Columbia and NW Venezuela.
Below: The Yellow-shouldered Amazon (Amazona barbadensis).

Yawning Amazons. Parrots yawn when they are tired, to take in oxygen, or simply to stretch their beaks. An Amazon pair often exhibits the same behavior gesture at the same time, as seen with this yawning twosome.

ner feeding, which now is observable particularly often. On the one hand it serves as an aggression-diminishing element to strengthen the pair bond; on the other, the male is trying out his inborn feeding mechanism. With pumping movements he regurgitates a stream of predigested food from his crop and tries to give this to the female. It sometimes takes a while before this process functions smoothly. Only if the food transfer works successfully, however, can it be guaranteed that later, during the brooding and raising of young, the female and the young birds will be able to receive nourishment from the male in sufficient amounts.

Copulation: The courtship period lasts only a few days, sometimes a few weeks; the female finally no longer avoids the male's attempts to get near her and invites mating with submissive posture and trembling, spread wings. With copulation the courtship period comes to an end, and a few days later, after successful egg laying, the female begins brooding. After 26 to 28 days the young appear.

How Amazons Threaten Opponents

Amazons live relatively peacefully with each other; great battles, which end with wounds or

still larger and more upright pose, he seeks the favor of the female, still more readily and aggressively attacks his aviary neighbors, and will be "egged on" by the loud, almost encouraging-sounding screams of the female. At this moment the display behavior is at its most striking. The female takes the wooing attempts of the male very coolly to begin with, and evades his attempts at copulation, at first growling strongly or resisting; with time, however, she suffers his approaches. The social preening creates diminished aggression and pair-bonding. It is an important component of courtship.

Partner feeding: Shortly before copulation yet another behavior appears, which, as with social preening, has a two-fold function: part-

Warning posture: With raised foot, the Amazon will first threaten his companion to drive him away from his place.

even death of the opponent, seldom occur. But since the space in an aviary is scarcely large enough for a courting and displaying Amazon male, fights there are not entirely out of the question. Smaller quarrels about food or rest and sleeping places are observable the whole year through. If one Amazon advances too close to another, he will threaten with a raised foot, to keep the "intruder" at a distance. If the threatened Amazon does not observe this "request," it can result in a regular footfight. Neither of the contestants will be wounded by this; the defeated one as a rule will yield his place after the quarrel. What looks threatening to the observer is the beak fight, in which the attacker directs his beak against the head, shoulders, and beak of the opponent, which the attacked one mostly parries. But both birds remain uninjured, because the natural social biting inhibition hinders serious biting, even though there are many chances to do so.

Note: If there are frequent conflicts between two Amazons over a long period of time, the keeper should separate the birds and try to place each of them with a different partner.

POPULAR AMAZON SPECIES

Some Facts About Amazons

Amazon parrots form a single genus among the nearly 9,700 species of living birds, which are grouped in approximately 330 genera, constituting the vertebrate class of birds.

Parrots are differentiated very distinctly from other bird groups by their body build, the curved beak, the toe position (two toes face forward, two rearward), and the grasping foot. Their closest relatives are the owls, the doves, and the cuckoos.

Parrots live in all parts of the earth with the exception of Europe. They dwell predominantly in the tropical and subtropical climate zones; only a few species live in barren regions, which are sought temporarily at times of frost or snowfall.

The Genus Amazona

The Amazon parrots were described scientifically for the first time by Lesson. They have the Latin genus name *Amazona*. To this group belong, according to some taxonomists, such as Joseph M. Forshaw and John and Pat Stoodley, 27 medium-large to large parrot species, which are mostly green in color and have a short, rounded tail. More recently, the 1990 book *Distribution and Taxonomy of Birds of*

The Lilac-crowned or Finsch's Amazon (Amazona finschi).

the World, by Charles G. Sibley and Burt L. Monroe Jr., identified 30 separate species within the genus *Amazona*. Of interest are two rather commonly known species; the double yellow-headed *(A. ochrocephala belizensis)* and the yellow-naped *(A. auropalliata)*. These two Amazons now have their own species identification instead of being listed as subspecies of the yellow-crowned Amazon *(A. ochrocephala)*. They are given allospecies status, since there is a lack of evidence that these three Amazons interbreed in areas where their geographical areas approach or overlap each other. Interesting in this respect is the fact that Dr. Marc Valenti clearly has shown through chromosomal analysis that the yellow-faced Amazon *(A. xanthops)* differs from all other Amazon species.

Range

Amazon parrots occur only in South and Central America, including the West Indies. In the north the distribution range of several species, such as the lilac-crowned *(A. finschi)*, white-fronted *(A. albifrons)*, green-cheeked *(A. viridigenalis)*, yellow-cheeked or red-crowned Amazons, extends up to Mexico and the borders of the United States. In the south the yellow-winged varieties of the blue-fronted Amazon reaches to northeastern Argentina and the northwestern tip of Uruguay. The majority of species are concentrated in the tropical climate zone between the northern and southern tropics. Their distribution range embraces a linear area from north to south of more than 3,000 miles (5,000 km).

Tropical forest climates with constant high temperatures and humidity as well as tropical savannah climates with short, dry periods characterize the regions in which Amazon parrots are at home.

Frequently Kept Amazon Species

In the past, almost all of the 27 or 30 Amazon species were imported to Europe and the United States at one time or another in more or less large numbers. Because of species protection laws, today only a few species are offered for sale, for example, orange-winged, blue-fronted, and Mealy Amazons. Other species, such as the yellow-crowned (*A. ochrocephala*), white-fronted (*A. albifrons*), green-cheeked (*A. viridigenalis*), lilac-crowned (*A. finschi*), and red-lored (*A. autumnalis*) Amazons, appear significantly less often in trade. All named species may—in accordance with the provisions of the animal protection laws—be bred in captivity. They are described in detail below.

Orange-winged Amazon
Amazona amazonica (3 subspecies)

Description: Total length 12–13 inches (30–33 cm); male and female: basic plumage color green; brow and crown irregularly blue-yellow; cheeks yellow; edges of wings yellow-green; wing speculum red; tail feathers green, the interiors of the outermost feathers partly red; beak horn-colored, darker at the tip; feet gray; unfeathered eye ring gray; iris yellow-orange. The young are similar to their parents, but the iris is grayish brown.

Range: All of northern South America with the exception of the Andes areas in the west and the coastal districts of eastern Brazil; in the south, in parts of Bolivia and in the northern tip of Paraguay.

Habitat: Damp woods and mangrove swamp areas. Also reported from urban areas and plantations.

Character: One of the best-known of all Amazon species. Easy to tame, teachable, but less "speech-gifted" species, which is good for keeping in a cage and also in an outdoor aviary, and is little prone to illness; in a roomy aviary several can be kept together, but can be rather noisy.

Breeding: Rather frequently bred; a breeder in Tampa, Florida, raised three chicks by hand in 1970. Clutch of three to four eggs, brooding time 25 days, nestling period eight to nine weeks; young birds are largely green, with only the beginnings of a few blue and yellow feathers in the head region.

Blue-fronted Amazon
Amazona aestiva (2 subspecies)

Description: Total length 14 inches (35 cm); male and female: basic plumage color green; forehead and bridle bright blue; crown, eye region, in some birds also the throat, breast front, and upper leg yellow; unfeathered eye ring gray-blue; front edge of wings red, usually shot through with yellow; wing speculum and tail feathers red at the base; beak black; feet blue-gray; iris red to orange. Immatures are duller than adults, with a reduced area of yellow and blue on the head. In the subspecies *Amazona aestiva xanthopteryx,* the edges of the wings are yellow, mixed with red, although in some birds the red is entirely replaced by yellow.

Range: The nominate form is in northeastern Brazil to Paraguay and the northern parts of Argentina; the variety *Amazona aestiva xanthopteryx* ranges from northern Bolivia, parts of southern Brazil, Paraguay, and northern Argentina to northernmost Buenos Aires.

Habitat: Preponderantly forests in tropical and subtropical climate zones.

Character: A popular species, known for decades. Easily tameable, good talent for imitation, but also makes natural sounds that are impossible to ignore; robust and hardy in cage and aviary. Frequently, behavioral changes occur with the onset of sexual maturity, particularly in single birds: increase in aggressiveness, courting, attempts to copulate, and false brooding in room cages; neurotic stereotypical movements, sometimes a tendency to feather picking.

Breeding: Frequently successful, but because of large numbers of imports in the past, still not much attempted. Several successful attempts were made a number of years ago. In spite of a positive outcome, however, there are by no means always breeding birds available in captivity. Sex determination is difficult, but adult females are likely to have red irises, males orange ones. Clutch of three to four eggs, brooding time 28 days, nestling time 55 to 60 days; several lutino-mutations have been documented. These birds are bright yellow, with white markings replacing the blue ones.

Mealy Amazon

Amazona farinosa (5 subspecies)

Description: Total length 15 to 15½ inches (38–40 cm). Male and female: basic plumage color green; upper side green, dusted with gray; some feathers on the crown are yellow; wing edges and speculum red; yellowish green band at the end of the tail; unfeathered eye ring white; beak a dark horn color with a yellow area at the base of the upper mandible; feet gray; iris red-brown. The variety *Amazona farinosa inornata* lacks the yellow on the crown area; the crown and the neck of the *Amazona farinosa guatemalae* are bluish.

Range: From Mexico in the north to the southern Atlantic coast of Brazil in the south; in the northwestern part of South America. *A. f. guatemalae* is from southern Mexico (Oaxaca and Veracruz) southward to Honduras. This subspecies is the most colorful member.

Habitat: Sparse rain forests and the forest border zone; thick tropical forests are largely shunned.

Character: At the moment this is probably the most commonly seen species in aviculture with a quiet, "harmonious" nature, comfortable movements, but piercing screams. It is extremely popular in the United States. It quickly becomes tame and gets along well with other Amazons. It is hardy, so it is well suited for outdoor aviary keeping.

Breeding: Until now scarcely successful; first German attempt *(Amazona farinosa guatemalae)* in 1984 by Dr. W. Burkhard, from Benningen, Germany; a clutch of three eggs was laid; brooding time 24–27 days, nestling period about 9–10 weeks.

Yellow-crowned or Yellow-fronted Amazon

Amazona ochrocephala (9 subspecies)

Description: Total length 13½ inches (35 cm); male and female; basic plumage color green; wing edge and wing speculum bright red; underside of tail yellowish green with a red spot at the base of each tail feather; beak dark gray, base and portion of upper mandible pink; feet gray; unfeathered eye ring white; iris orange.

Range: South America from the Guyanas and Venezuela in the east to the Colombian Andes in the west; island of Trinidad.

Amazona ochrocephala panamensis resembles the nominate form but the forehead is yellow, the beak is horn-colored with a darker point on the upper mandible, the feet are flesh-colored; it is smaller (13 inches [33 cm]).

Range: Western Panama and the tropical lowlands in northern Colombia.

The Yellow-crowned Amazon (Amazona ochrocephala).

Amazona ochrocephala auropalliata resembles the nominate form, except the nape portion is yellow, the upper mandible is gray, the lower mandible horn-colored gray, the eye ring is gray, the feet flesh-colored; it is larger (15 inches [39 cm]).

Range: Central America, from southwestern Mexico in the north to Costa Rica in the south.

Amazona ochrocephala oratrix resembles the nominate form except the head and nape are yellow, the beak is horn-colored, the feet are brighter; it is larger (16 inches [41 cm]).

Range: Mexico.

Amazona ochrocephala belizensis resembles the *oratrix* subspecies except for a less extensive area of yellow on the head.

Range: Honduras.

Top: The Blue-fronted Amazon (Amazona aestiva).
Bottom: The Green-cheeked Amazon (Amazona viridigenalis).

The other subspecies occur singly or are unknown in the trade.

Some of the more frequently kept varieties have acquired their own English names:

✔ *Amazona ochrocephala ochrocephala:* Surinam Amazon

✔ *Amazona ochrocephala panamensis:* Panama yellow-headed Amazon

✔ *Amazona ochrocephala auropalliata:* Yellow-naped or Golden-naped Amazon

✔ *Amazona ochrocephala oratrix:* Double yellow-fronted or Mexican yellow-headed Amazon; and *Amazona ochrocephala belizensis:* Double yellow-headed Amazon of British Honduras.

Character: Rarely imported now, but, because of large quantities imported in earlier days, seen very frequently all over. Robust, hardy cage and aviary birds; all varieties are easy to tame and possess an extraordinary talent for mimicry but also a very loud natural voice that manifests itself even more strongly during the mating period.

Breeding: Often successful with a number of varieties. Clutches of three to four eggs, brooding time 26 to 28 days, nestling period 9–11 weeks.

White-fronted or White-browed Amazon, or Spectacled Amazon

Amazona albifrons (3 subspecies)

Description: This is the smallest of all Amazon species and less raucous than its larger relatives; total length 10 inches (26 cm); male: basic plumage color green; forehead white; crown green-blue; eye area and bridle red; unfeathered eye ring gray-white; wing edges red; beak yellowish; legs bright gray; iris yellowish; female: resembles the male but without the red wing edge (alula); the primary coverts are green. Immature males have a green alula and the white color of the forehead and forecrown is tinged with yellow.

Range: From the west coast of Mexico across Guatemala, Honduras, El Salvador, Nicaragua to Costa Rica.

Habitat: Dry bush and deciduous forests up to about 1,800 m (6,000 ft); only occasionally tropical rain forest areas.

Character: Very common in aviculture as they are relatively quiet and easily sexed by sight, although females are always in the minority. Young birds are, as already stated, recognizable by a dark iris and above all by the yellowish color on the forehead instead of white. Kept singly they should quickly become tame and reveal a noteworthy "speaking ability;" kept in an aviary they are mostly shy and fearful; in a roomy aviary they are skillful fliers.

Breeding: Males and females are differentiated in color. There has been successful breeding by several parrot fanciers including many in the United States; clutches of three to four, and in exceptional cases five eggs; length of brooding 24–26 days; nestling period about 52–56 days.

Green-cheeked or Red-crowned Amazon

Amazona viridigenalis

Sometimes known as Mexican red-headed Amazon.

Description: Total length 13 inches (33 cm); male and female: basic plumage color green; forehead and crown red (less extensive in females); half-moon-shaped blue-violet band in the cheek area; primary coverts blue and red; beak yellowish, with white cere; unfeathered eye ring white; legs gray; iris yellow. Immatures: Crown green; only lores and forehead are red. The violet-blue markings are less extensive and duller.

Range: Northeastern Mexico exclusively; there is a small feral population near Los Angeles.

Habitat: Forest areas along rivers, grain-cultivating districts in damp lowlands, sparse, dry, pine-covered mountain ridges, tropical forests of the canyons.

Character: Were often available during the 1970s and 1980s, and a great number of true pairs are now well established in collections. Usually animals come into trade from private hands and among them are some captive-bred birds. Less suitable for keeping in a cage, where single birds are very inactive; also in an outdoor aviary less lively than other species; have piercing cries.

Breeding: Adult males and females are clearly differentiated because of the different dimensions of the red head patch that is less extensive in the female. First breeding in 1970 in Africa and England; clutch two to three eggs, brooding period 28 days, nestling period about 70 days, independent eating at about 120 days.

Lilac-crowned or Finsch's Amazon

Amazona finschi (2 subspecies)

Description: Total length 13 inches (33 cm); male and female: basic plumage color green, neck and upper side with black margins; forehead and bridle red-brown; crown, neck, and half-moon around cheek feathers bluish white; wings blue-black; beak horn-colored; feet gray; iris orange. Immatures: Slightly duller; iris brownish; skin surrounding the eyes and cere white.

Range: Western Mexico.

Habitat: Plains, forested mountain regions up to heights of about 7,200 feet (2,200 m), occasionally in grain fields and banana plantations.

Character: Last large import around 1980; no more imported since. In behavior similar to the green-cheeked Amazon (*A. viridigenalis*), but livelier; very nimble flier; less suited for keeping in a cage, although young birds can become tame.

Breeding: Many attempts at artificial breeding and hand-feeding have been successful in the United States, England, the Netherlands, and Germany; brooding time 26 days; nestling period around 54 to 60 days.

Red-lored or Primrose-cheeked Amazon

Amazona autumnalis (4 subspecies)

Description: Total length 13½ inches (34 cm); male and female: basic plumage color green; forehead and bridle scarlet red; crown and individual neck feathers bright blue; cheeks yellow; wing speculum red; wing pinion blue-black; beak dark horn-colored; feet gray; unfeathered eye ring white; iris gold-brown to dark brown; the subspecies *Amazona autumnalis salvini* (Salvin's Amazon) lacks the yellow cheek color and is somewhat larger than the nominate; in *Amazona autumnalis lilacina* (Ecuador Amazon) the crown is blue-violet, the ear region green, the beak whitish and gray; *Amazona autumnalis diadema* (diademed Amazon) resembles Salvin's Amazon but differs from it mainly in the thick, red, hairlike feathers of the nose area.

Range: The nominate form along the east coast of Mexico to the peninsula of Belize,

The Festive Amazon (Amazona festiva).

The Cuban Amazon (Amazona leucocephala).

Guatemala, and Honduras; *Amazona autumnalis salvini* in Nicaragua, Costa Rica, Panama, and the west coast of Colombia; *Amazona autumnalis lilacina* only in Western Ecuador; *Amazona autumnalis diadema* in interior Brazil.

Habitat: Tropical lowland forests and forest border zones.

Character: Red-lored Amazons appear occasionally, Salvin's and Ecuador Amazons very seldom, and diademed Amazons never in the trade; the occasional birds available are mostly from private owners. All known varieties get used to cage and aviary living well; they are easily tamed and have an agreeable manner. Their "speaking ability" is not particularly large; their own cries are piercing and monotonous.

Breeding: Only isolated successes; first successful attempt with the Ecuador Amazon in 1946 in the United States, with the nominate form in 1956 in England; clutches of three eggs; brooding time 26 to 28 days, no exact details about nestling periods, but should be approximately 8–9 weeks.

The Red-crowned Amazon (Amazona rhodocorytha).

A P P E N D I X

Parrot Species in Danger of Extinction

Appendix I of the Washington Convention lists all the parrots that are in immediate danger of extinction or close to it. Trade in these birds is prohibited except for parrots that were raised in captivity. The most recent edition of Appendix I, drawn up in 1997, includes the following species.

Amazona arausiaca, Red-necked Amazon

Amazona barbadensis, Yellow-shouldered Amazon

Amazona brasiliensis, Red-tailed Amazon

Amazona collaria, Yellow-billed Amazon

Amazona dufresniana rhodocorytha, Red-crowned Amazon

Amazona finschi, Lilac-crowned Amazon

Amazona guildingii, St. Vincent Amazon

Amazona imperialis, Imperial Amazon

Amazona leucocephala, Cuban Amazon

Amazona oratrix, Yellow-headed Amazon

Amazona pretrei, Red-spectacled Amazon

Amazona rhodocorytha, Red-browed Amazon

Amazona tucumana, Tucuman Amazon

Amazona ventralis, Hispaniolan Amazon

Amazona versicolor, Versicolor or St. Lucia Amazon

Amazona vinacea, Vinaceous Amazon

Amazona viridigenalis, Green-cheeked Amazon

Amazona vittata, Puerto Rican Amazon

Amazona xanthops, Yellow-faced Amazon

Anodorhynchus glaucus, Glaucous Macaw (may be extinct)

Anodorhynchus leari, Lear's Macaw

Ara ambigua, Great Green Macaw

Ara glaucogularis, Blue-throated Macaw

Ara macao, Scarlet Macaw

Ara rubrogenys, Red-fronted or Red-crowned Macaw

Aratinga guarouba, Golden Conure

Cyanopsitta spixii, Spix's Macaw

Cyanoramphus auriceps forbesi, subspecies of Yellow-fronted Parakeet

Cyanoramphus novaezelandiae, Red-fronted Parakeet

Pyrrhura cruentata, Red-eared Conure

Rhynchopsitta spp., Thick-billed Parrots (two races)

Strigops habroptilus, Owl Parrot or Kakapo

Trichlaria malachitaeea, Purple-bellied Parrot

Extinct Species

A number of parrots became extinct during the eighteenth and nineteenth centuries. The reasons are not known, but change in and destruction of the parrots' natural habitat have been blamed as well as shooting the birds for food and catching them for the pet trade. The following list contains all the species that are known to have existed, and in parentheses is the date when they presumably died out.

Amazona vittata gracilipes, subspecies of Puerto Rican Amazon (1899)

Ara tricolor, Cuban Macaw (1885)

Aratinga chloroptera maugei, Mauge's Conure (ca. 1860)

Charmosyna diadema, New Caledonian Lorikeet (ca. 1860)

Conuropsis carolinensis carolinensis, Carolina Parakeet (ca. 1900)

Conuropsis carolinensis ludovicianus, subspecies of the above (1914)

Cyanoramphus novaezelandiae erythrotis, subspecies of Red-footed Parakeet (1800–1820)

Cyanoramphus novaezelandiae subflavescens, subspecies of Red-fronted Parakeet (ca. 1870)

Cyanoramphus ulietanus, Society Parakeet (1773/4)

Cyanoramphus zealandicus, Black-footed Parakeet (1844)

Loriculus philippensis chrysonotus, subspecies of Philippine Hanging Parrot (after 1926)

Mascarinus mascarinus, Mascarene Parrot (1800–1820)

Nest or meridionalis productus, Norfolk Island Kaka (1851)

Psittacula eupatria wardi, Seychelles Parakeet (ca. 1870)

Psittacula exsul, Newton's Parakeet (ca. 1875)

INFORMATION

American Bird Clubs

Amazona Society
10609 264th Street East
Graham, WA 98338
(253) 847-1314

American Federation of Aviculture (AFA)
P.O. Box 56218
Phoenix, AZ 85079-6218
(602) 484-0931
Fax: (602) 484-0109
E-mail: stat@wizard.net

Bird Clubs of America
P.O. Box 2005
Yorktown, VA 23692
(804) 898-5090, or
414 Windmill Avenue
West Babylon, NY 11704
(516) 587-5739

International Aviculturists Society
P.O. Box 280383
Memphis, TN 38168
(901) 872-7612

Parrot Rehabilitation Society
P.O. Box 620213
San Diego, CA 92102-0213
(619) 283-8015, or
Bob Plymesser (619) 224-6546

Canadian Bird Clubs

Avicultural Advancement Council
P.O. Box 5126
Postal Station "B"
Victoria, British Columbia V8R 6N4

British Columbia Avicultural Society
c/o Mr. Paul Prior
11784-90th Avenue
North Delta, British Columbia V4C 3H6

Calgary and District Avicultural Society
c/o Mr. Richard Kary
7728 Bowcliffe Cr., N.W.
Calgary, Alberta T3B 2S5

Canadian Parrot Association
Pine Oaks, R.R. Nr. 3
St. Catherines, Ontario L2R 6P9

Books

Birmelin, I., and A. Wolter. *The New Parakeet Handbook.* Hauppauge, New York: Barron's Educational Series, 1985.
Cayley N. W., and A. Lendon. *Australian Parrots in Field and Aviary.* Sydney, Australia: Angus & Robertson, 1973.
Diemer, P. *Parrots.* Hauppauge, New York: Barron's Educational Series, 1983.
Eastman, W. R., and A. C. Hunt. *The Parrots of Australia.* Sydney, Australia: Angus & Robertson, 1966.

The Yellow-crowned Amazon (**Amazona ochrocephala**).

Forshaw, J. M. *Australian Parrots,* 2nd edition. Melbourne, Australia: Lansdowne Press, 1981.

——. *Parrots of the World,* 3rd edition. Melbourne, Australia: Lansdowne Press, 1989.

Harman, I. *Australian Parrots in Bush and Aviary.* Melbourne and Sydney, Australia: Inkata Press, 1981.

Hoppe, D. *The World of Amazon Parrots.* Neptune, New Jersey: TFH Publications, 1985.

Juniper, T., and M. Parr. Parrots. *A Guide to Parrots of the World.* New Haven and London: Yale University Press, 1998.

Lantermann, W. *The New Parrot Handbook.* Hauppauge, New York: Barron's Educational Series, 1986.

Low, R. *The Complete Book of Parrots.* Hauppauge, New York: Barron's Educational Series, 1989.

——. *Endangered Parrots.* Poole, Dorset, England: Blandford Press, 1980.

——. *Parrots, Their Care and Breeding.* Poole, Dorset, England: Blandford Press, 1980.

Moizer, S. and B. *The Complete Book of Budgerigars.* Hauppauge, New York: Barron's Educational Series, 1988.

Petrak, M. L. *Diseases of Cage and Aviary Birds,* 2nd edition. Philadelphia, Pennsylvania: Lea & Febiger, 1982.

Ruthers, A., and K. A. Norris. *Encyclopedia of Aviculture,* Vol. 2. Poole, Dorset, England: Blandford Press, 1972.

Vriends, M. M. *Hand-feeding and Raising Baby Birds,* Hauppauge, New York: Barron's Educational Series, 1996.

——. *Popular Parrots,* 2nd edition. New York: Howell Book House, Inc., 1984.

——. *Simon and Schuster's Guide to Pet Birds.* New York: Simon and Schuster, 1986.

Wolter, A. *African Gray Parrots.* Hauppauge, New York: Barron's Educational Series, 1987.

Periodicals

Avicultural Bulletin (Monthly)
Avicultural Society of America, Inc.
P.O. Box 2796
Redondo Beach, CA 90278

Avicultural Magazine (Quarterly)
The Avicultural Society
Windsor, Forest Stud, Mill Ride
Ascot, Berkshire, England

Bird Talk (Monthly)
P.O. Box 57347
Boulder, CO 80323-7347
Phone (800) 365-4421
Fax (303) 604-7455

Cage and Aviary Birds (Weekly)
Prospect House
9-15 Ewell Road
Cheam, Sutton, Surrey, SM3 8BZ, England

Young birdkeepers under 16 may want to join the *Junior Bird League;* full details can be obtained from the J.B.L., c/o *Cage and Aviary Birds.*

Magazine of the Parrot Society (Monthly)
19a De Parys Avenue
Bedford, Bedfordshire, England

Watchbird (Bi-monthly)
American Federation of Aviculture
P.O. Box 56218
Phoenix, AZ 85079-6218
Phone (602) 484-0931
Fax (602) 484-0109

Acclimation, 25–26
Activities, 28–29
Age determination, 11
Amazona:
  aestiva, 74–75, 77
  albifrons, 68, 78
  amazonica, 20, 33, 40, 74
  arausiaca, 44
  autumnalis, 79–80
    salvini, 33
  barnadensis, 12, 57, 69
  farinosa, 75
  festiva, 41
    bodini, 81
  finschi, 69, 72, 79
  genus, 73
  guildingii, 32
  imperialis, 24
  leucocephala, 4, 21, 80
  ochrocephala, 8, 12, 16, 21,
    49, 57, 64, 69, 76, 76, 78
    panamensis, 36, 52
  oratrix, 21
  pretrei, 12
  range, 73–74
  tucumana, 80
  ventralis, 29
  vinacea, 13
  viridigenalis, 77, 78–79
  xanthops, 49
Amazons:
  breeding, 53–63
  care of, 34–35
  common illnesses of, 45–49
  and other pets, 7
  play and activities, 28–29
  purchase considerations
    before, 5–6
  serious threats to, 15
  species frequently kept,
    74–80
  speech training, 27–28
Appearance, 10
Aspergillosis, 47
Aviary, 17–18, 26, 35

Beak shortening, 34–35
Behavior, 10
  in wild, 65–67, 70–71
Bill, 11
Bird clubs, list of, 84
Bird shows, 62–63
Blue-fronted Amazon, 74–75,
  77
Bodin's Amazon, 81
Books, list of, 84–85
Breeders, 9
Breeding:
  bird shows, 62–63
  courtship and mating, 56

egg laying and brooding, 56
food for, 39, 56–59, 61
hand-feeding, 58–59, 61
hatching and rearing young,
  57–58
hybrids, 61–62
legal requirements for, 54
maintenance conditions for,
  54–56
for species preservation,
  53–54
Breeding period, 65
Brooding, 56

Cage, 17, 35
Care, 34–35
Chicks, 58–59, 61
Children, 7
CITES, 5
Claws, cutting, 34
Cleaning housing, 35
Climbing, 66
Climbing trees, 22
Coccidiosis, 47
Copulation, 47
Courtship behavior, 56, 67, 70
Crop inflammation, 47
Cuban Amazon, 4, 21, 80

Dangers, list of, 30–31
Diet, 37–39, 42–43, 56–59, 61,
  66
Diseases, 45–49
Display behavior, 67, 70
Drinking containers, 18–19
Drinking water, 42

Ectoparasites, 45
Egg laying, 56, 65
Endangered species, list of,
  82–83
Endoparasites, 45–46
Endoscopy, 14
Exhibitions, 62–63
External sex characteristics, 14
Eyes, 11

Feather chromosome sexing, 14
Feather eating/picking, 48–49
Feces, 10, 25
Females, 11, 14
Festive Amazon, 41
Fighting behavior, 70–71
Finsch's Amazon, 69, 72, 79
First aid, 50
Flight cage, 23, 35
Food, 37–39, 42–43, 56–59, 61,
  66
Food containers, 18–19
Free flight, 29

Freestanding perches, 22
Fruit, 38

Green-cheeked Amazon, 77,
  78–79
Green feed, 38–39
Group size, 65

Hand-feeding, 58–59, 61
Hand-taming, 26–27
Hatching, 57
Hispaniolan Amazon, 29
Housing:
  cage, 17
  cleaning, 35
  fittings for cages and room
    aviaries, 18–19
  freestanding perches and
    climbing trees, 19, 22
  outdoor shelter and flight
    cage, 22–23
  room aviaries, 17–18
Hybrids, 61–62

Illnesses, 45–49
Imperial Amazon, 24
Incubation problems, 57–58
Infrared heat, 50
Intestinal inflammation, 46

Legs, 11
Lilac-crowned Amazon, 69, 72,
  79

Males, 11, 14
Mating, 56
Mealy Amazon, 75
Mimicking ability, 28
Minerals, 42

Nest boxes, 55
Newcastle disease, 15
Nutrition, 37–39, 42–43,
  56–59, 61, 66
Nutritional condition, 11

Orange-winged Amazon, 20,
  33, 40, 74
Outdoor climbing trees, 22
Outdoor shelter, 22–23

Pair bonding, 65
Pairs, 6–7, 54–55
Panama Amazon, 36, 52
Parasites, 45–46
Parrot fever (psittacosis), 49
Partner feeding, 70
Pellets, 39
Perches, 18, 22
Periodicals, list of, 85

Pet stores, 9
Play, 28–29
Plumage, 11
Preening, 66–67
Primrose-cheeked Amazon,
  79–80
Protein, 39

Quarantine, 9

Rearing young, 57–58, 66
Red-crowned Amazon, 78–79
Red-lored Amazon, 33, 79–80
Red-necked Amazon, 44
Red-spectacled Amazon, 12
Respiratory ailments, 47–48
Room aviary, 17–18

St. Vincent Amazon, 32
Salmonellosis, 46
Seeds, 37
Sex determination, 11, 14
Shower bath, 34
Sickness, signs of, 50
Single bird, 6
Size, 11
Smuggled birds, 15
Social preening, 66–67
Species:
  endangered, list of, 82–83
  extinct, list of, 83
  frequently kept, 74–80
  preservation of, 53–54
Spectacled Amazon, 78
Speech training, 27–28
Sprouted feed, 37–38
Sunflower seeds, 37

Table scraps, 39
Tame parrot, 27
Temperature requirements, 55–56
Toes, 11
Toys, 19, 29
Transport box, 25–26
Trichomoniasis, 46–47
Tucuman Amazon, 80

Veterinarian, 51
Vinaceous Amazon, 13
Vitamins, 39

Washington Endangered
  Species Convention, 53
White-fronted (-browed)
  Amazon, 68, 78
Wings, 11

Yellow-crowned (-fronted)
  Amazon, 8, 12, 16, 21, 49,
  57, 64, 69, 76, 78

About the Authors

Werner Lantermann has been director of a private institute for parrot research in Oberhausen, Germany since 1981. His special interest centers on the large parrots of Central and South America. He is the author of numerous articles in professional journals and of successful books about parrot keeping and breeding, among them Barron's *The New Parrot Handbook.*

Susanne Lantermann is Werner Lantermann's co-worker in the private institute for parrot research in Oberhausen and coauthor of various books about African and South American parrots.

Dr. Matthew M. Vriends is a well-known biologist/aviculturist and author of more than 100 books.

Photo Credits

Angermayer: page 33; Skogstad: page 68; Vriends: front cover, back cover, inside front cover, inside back cover, pages 3, 4, 12, 13, 16, 20, 21, 24, 28, 29, 32, 36, 37, 40, 41, 44, 49, 52, 57, 60, 69, 72, 76, 77, 80, 81, 84; Wothe: pages 8 and 64.

Additional Drawing Tanya Heming-Vriends: page 51.

Important Note

People who suffer from allergies to feathers or any kind of feather dust should not keep parrots. In case of doubt, check with the doctor before you acquire one.

In dealing with parrots, one may receive injuries from bites or scratches. Have such wounds attended to by a doctor. Although psittacosis (parrot fever) is not among the commonly seen illnesses of parrots (see page 45), it can produce symptoms in both humans and parrots that may be life-threatening. At any sign of a cold or flu (see page 50), see a doctor immediately.

English language edition © copyright 2000 by Barron's Educational Series, Inc.
Prior edition © copyright 1988 by Barron's Educational Series, Inc.
© Copyright 1987 by Gräfe und Unzer GmbH, Munich, Germany
Original German title is *Amazonen*
Translated from the German by Elizabeth D. Crawford

All rights reserved.
No part of this book may be reproduced in any form, by photostat, microfilm, xerography, or any other means, or incorporated into any information retrieval system, electronic or mechanical, without the written permission of the copyright owner.

All inquiries should be addressed to:
Barron's Educational Series, Inc.
250 Wireless Boulevard
Hauppauge, NY 11788
http://www.barronseduc.com

Library of Congress Catalog Card No. 99-51772
ISBN-13: 978-0-7641-1036-8
ISBN-10: 0-7641-1036-5
Library of Congress Cataloging-in-Publication Data
Lantermann, Werner, 1956–
    [Amazonen. English].
    Amazon parrots / Werner and Susanne Lantermann ; advisory editor, Matthew M. Vriends ; with color photographs by well-known animal photographers and illustrations by Fritz W. Kohler.
        p. cm.
    Includes bibliographical references.
    ISBN 0-7641-1036-5
    1. Amazon parrots. I. Lantermann, Susanne.
II. Vriends, Matthew M., 1937– . III. Title.
SF473.P3 L3513   2000
636.6'865—dc21   99-51772
                                  CIP

Printed in China

19 18 17 16 15 14 13 12